Silvia Schultermandl, Jana Aresin, Si Sophie Pages Whybrew, Dijana Simić (eds.)
Affective Worldmaking

Gender Studies

Stories bring us together, untold stories keep us apart.
–Elif Shafak

Silvia Schultermandl (she/her), born in 1977, is a professor and chair of American studies at Westfälische Wilhelms-Universität Münster. She researches various themes in transnational studies, American literature and culture, as well as family and kinship studies.

Jana Aresin (she/her), born in 1992, is a doctoral researcher in American studies at Friedrich-Alexander Universität Erlangen-Nürnberg. She researches the cultural and media history of the early Cold War (1945-1960) in comparative perspective, with a regional focus on the United States and Japan. In 2020-21 she was Elisabeth-List Junior Fellow at the Coordination Centre for Gender Studies and Equal Opportunity at Karl-Franzens-Universität Graz.

Si Sophie Pages Whybrew (she/her, they/them), born in 1987, is a senior scientist for gender and diversity studies at Kunst-Universität Graz. They completed their dissertation on "Affective Trans Worldmaking in Contemporary Science Fiction" at Karl-Franzens-Universität Graz. From 2020-21, they were an Elisabeth-List Junior Fellow at the Coordination Centre for Gender Studies in the research project "Literary Negotiations of Affective and Gendered Belongings."

Dijana Simić (she/her), born in 1988, is a lecturer of Bosnian, Croatian, and Serbian literary and cultural studies in the Department of Slavic Studies at Karl-Franzens-Universität Graz. Currently, she is completing her PhD project on gender, sexuality, and intimate counterpublics in recent Bosnian-Herzegovinian prose. Her teaching and research focus on migration, gender, and memory studies in the former Yugoslav context.

Silvia Schultermandl, Jana Aresin,
Si Sophie Pages Whybrew, Dijana Simić (eds.)

Affective Worldmaking

Narrative Counterpublics of Gender and Sexuality

Bibliographic information published by the Deutsche Nationalbibliothek
The Deutsche Nationalbibliothek lists this publication in the Deutsche National-
bibliografie; detailed bibliographic data are available in the Internet at http://
dnb.d-nb.de

First published in 2022 by transcript Verlag, Bielefeld
© Silvia Schultermandl, Jana Aresin, Si Sophie Pages Whybrew, Dijana Simić (eds.)

Cover layout: Maria Arndt, Bielefeld
Cover illustration: Silvia Schultermandl

Print-ISBN 978-3-8376-6141-5
PDF-ISBN 978-3-8394-6141-9
https://doi.org/10.14361/9783839461419
ISSN of series: 2625-0128
eISSN of series: 2703-0482

Contents

Senses of Affective Worldmaking

Counternarratives and Community Building

Foreword

This edited collection is the result of a collaborative research project entitled "Intimate Readings: Literary Negotiations of Affective and Gendered Belongings," funded by the Elisabeth-List-Fellowship Program at the University of Graz. Our project, akin to this book, was designed to facilitate conversations about the valence of affect theory for a better understanding of how narratives of gender and sexuality can depict and foster a sense of belonging. Through our systematic investigation of the intersections between affect theory and literary theory, we found that narratives across different media employ unique strategies of affective interpellation, on the level of representation as well as on the level of reception. We have come to think of this as affective worldmaking. In this collection, we present the results of our theorizations on these intersections, alongside a collection of essays by a diverse range of scholars who explore the potential for and limitations of affective worldmaking in various forms and modes of narration through the lens of their respective disciplinary, theoretical, cultural, and political backgrounds. In the process, they invite us to reflect on different modes of affective worldmaking as well as potential disciplinary challenges and competing concepts that arise from and in their respective fields of study or current research areas.

In this way, this collection represents both an outgrowth and extension of our collaboration and of the affective and intellectual impulses and insights that emerged in the course of our online symposium "Affective Worldmaking: Narrative Counterpublics of Gender and Sexuality" (January 14th-15th, 2021), during which we had the chance to discuss our ideas with many of the contributors to this volume. Indeed, the affective and intellectual momentum of this symposium also reverberates throughout the radio series "Gender, Affect, and Politics," which we produced for the show *genderfrequenz* (Gender Frequency), of the Graz-based independent radio station Radio Helsinki. You can access the series by using the QR code in the final chapter. We are grateful for the opportunity to use their airwaves to present our discussions of affective worldmaking in the context of gender discrimination, misogyny, homophobia, and transphobia to an audience outside of our academic bubble and for the chance this offered us to practice a little affective worldmaking ourselves.

In a similar vein, this edited collection has been a worldmaking endeavor in its own right. During the societal, social, and interpersonal upheaval of the COVID-19 pandemic, this project allowed us to establish and reinvigorate new and existing interrelationships between affect and literary studies and discover new ways of affective worldmaking both on a theoretical and an interpersonal level. And like the pandemic itself, it has required everybody involved to deal with unfamiliar terrain seemingly far-removed from habitual grooves. That being said, affective worldmaking also gained another dimension of meaning for us during the pandemic. As scholars of affect theory, we could not help but notice how our own lived experiences and practices changed, how the pace and sequence of our discussion meetings and the feelings of community that arose through them shifted and morphed, as we were forced to adopt new, socially distanced forms of working together. Indeed, what began as a project conceived in cozy Austrian cafés and envisioned as a series of social events with local and international collaborators was unexpectedly transformed into online encounters and occasional, socially distanced coffee meetings in the frosty backyards of Graz, an experience that was both marked by stasis and uncertainty, over- and underwhelmedness, distance, and intimacy, both in our academic routines and personal interactions. Thus, our collaborative efforts were, to a large extent, characterized by our desire to *do* affective worldmaking in our own contexts and put our ideas about its potentials into practice, both in our personal and professional lives, in order to make sense of our experiences and emotions and to reclaim moments of connection and commonality.

The beginnings of our project and the onset of the pandemic coincided. Yet, in addition to voicing our frustrations with this new experience of isolation, our meetings and discussions also became spaces of productive encounter and healing that broke the monotony of social distancing, thereby opening up new opportunities for connection, in the spirit of affect studies' tradition of "reparative practice," both within our research group and with our collaborators, as we edited their texts and recognized, empathized, and shared their frustrations and anxieties in the face of these unforeseen circumstances. At the same time, however, we found relief in their honesty and vulnerability.

In the spirit of honesty, vulnerability, and connection, we would like to take this opportunity to not only thank both institutions but especially the people who supported and worked with us under these uncertain circumstances to turn this project into a wonderful communal journey of affective and intellectual exploration. We want to thank the University of Graz and especially the Coordination Center for Gender Studies and Equal Opportunities for funding our project: in particular, Barbara Hey and Lisa Scheer for their gracious and invaluable logistical and personal support in making this project a reality, promoting our research, and their tireless support of gender and sexuality studies at the University of Graz. We are also indebted to Diana Brunnthaler for lending us her audio-editing and suturing skills for our radio series and making us sound better than we could have ever imagined, as well as to Aline Franzus and Chris Wahlig for their editorial work on this collection, especially their careful reading and meticulous formatting.

Introduction: Affective Worldmaking: Narrative Counterpublics of Gender and Sexuality

Silvia Schultermandl, Jana Aresin, Dijana Simić and Si Sophie Pages Why-brew

"In losing our voice, something in us dies" (9), writes award-winning British-Turkish writer, storyteller, essayist, academic, public speaker, and activist Elif Shafak in *How to Stay Sane in an Age of Division* (2020). Shafak emphasizes the importance of telling one's story as a means of restoring agency over one's life. While the COVID-19 pandemic, during which her book was published, lends a particular urgency to this imperative, her notion of the valence of story-sharing highlights the significance of storytelling as a personal, social, cultural, and political practice. Shafak's meditation on the need for stories outside the mainstream discourse is prompted by her observation of a trans woman who walks by Shafak's Istanbul apartment late at night: she is visibly physically hurt but resiliently and defiantly belts the experience of her abuse into the night. It is this particular act of witnessing which inspires Shafak's musings: "To be deprived of a voice means to be deprived of agency over our own lives. It also means to slowly but systematically become alienated from our own journeys, struggles and inner transformations, and begin to view even our most subjective experiences as though through someone else's eyes, and external gaze" (8).

Therefore, in Shafak's poetic description, storytelling is an integral part of our identity: "We are made of stories—those that have happened, those that are still happening at this moment in time, and those that are shaped purely in our imagination through words, images, dreams and an endless sense of wonder about the world around us and how it works. Unvarnished truths, innermost reflections, fragments of memory, wounds healed" (9). Everyone's story matters. Stories that depict the lives and experiences of marginalized individuals and their communities are of particular importance, as they are often not present within dominant discourses. By creating visibility for underrepresented communities, stories also provide an occasion for readers to engage with these perspectives, experiences, and worldviews. As Shafak contends, "[t]he moment when we stop listening to diverse opinions is also when we stop learning. Because the truth is we don't learn much from sameness and monotony. We usually learn from differences" (16). Shafak summarizes this in the following aphorism, quoted in our book's epigraph: "Stories bring us together, untold stories keep us apart" (9).

Shafak's astute observations about the power of storytelling offer interesting starting points for a theorization of the worldmaking capacity of narratives. In *Affective Worldmaking: Narrative Counterpublics of Gender and Sexuality*, we start from the understanding that lived experiences are mediated, negotiated, and demarcated through language and narrative storytelling. Narratives are not restricted to literature but also shape and structure public discourse through various media and text forms. Indeed, dominant narratives have a significant impact on constructions of individual and collective identities, on whose identities are deemed comprehensible and are thus (in)validated, who gets to be a subject, how people position themselves in the world, and how they recover untold pasts, call attention to marginalized presents, and imagine possible futures for themselves.

Cultural and communal practices of marginalized groups have often been sidelined in dominant cultural narratives. They have even been met with hostility and discrimination. Marginalized communities have often responded to this violence by using and creating different forms of cultural production, media, institutions, and spaces to develop discourses of their own, to express themselves, to connect with each other, and to question hegemonic conceptions of, among others, race, ethnicity, class, gender, sexuality, and dis/ability. As Shafak's example illustrates, these narratives engender new feelings, observations, and musings. Michael Warner conceptualizes this process as the creation of counterpublics through the circulation of discourses (Warner 65–66). These text-based counterpublics offer possibilities for conceiving alternatives to hegemonic narratives, and thus they can be understood as worldmaking projects.

Both in academia and wider public and political discourses, the relation between affect, emotion, identity, and belonging has been receiving increased interest. Particularly in the face of widespread feelings of crisis, growing from heightened political and socio-economic divides, the rise of right-wing politics, neo-conservatism, and a crisis of trust in political and intellectual elites, news media, and science, the question of what shapes people's individual and collective identities, what makes them feel they belong, and how these processes make use of particular narratives and appeal to emotional and affective structures has gathered new attention. *Affective Worldmaking* contributes to these conversations through three lines of inquiry that are present in all the contributing chapters, as they engage with literary and cultural narratives beyond questions of rhetoric, discourse, and representation. The first line of inquiry focuses on the level of texts' affective dimensions and the protagonists' experiences, relationships, and emotions. The second focuses on the reader and theorizes the affective attachments readers may form to texts. And finally, the third line of inquiry focuses on the context by considering the potential for societal and political transformation. All three lines are interconnected; by delineating their respective facets separately, we want to throw into relief the multiple layers of meaning affective worldmaking can have.

The first line of inquiry considers how texts' affective narrative strategies form bases for identification and belonging amongst protagonists and to what extent they offer potential points of recognition to audiences. Regarding the narratives' formal and aesthetic dimensions, we explore how particular affective experiences of the depicted worlds enable what this volume calls 'affective worldmaking,' and to what degree established canonical and genre traditions play a role in this. With the example of Shafak's use of a collective *we*, one might ask: Whom does her we-narration include, whom does it potentially exclude? How does her use of the first-person plural affectively interpellate readers? What does a "we" look like that honors individual positionalities and subjectivities, as they are shaped by unique experiences, desires, and beliefs, while still indexing a sense of communal or collective agency and accountability?

The second line of inquiry addresses the level of affective experience when engaging with narratives of gender and sexuality. This places the focus on readers' interactions with these narratives and their participation in the kinds of affective worldmaking that occurs. We think of readers here not as instances within the text, as is common in reader-response theory, but as "sentient beings" (Schultermandl 13) who respond to narratives in unique ways. Shafak's narrative revolves around her simultaneous experience of feelings of solidarity with the woman she sees and her feeling of guilt for not actively asking her whether she was alright. Nevertheless, the encounter Shafak describes seems well etched into her memory and still resonates years later when she is already living in London. Regarding narratives' potential to do something to and with us, we ask: Which affective responses do the narratives' discussions of cultural traditions, community practices, and kinship rituals elicit, and how may they contribute to the audiences' sense of belonging? Going beyond the scope of individual affective responses, we also attend to narratives' potential to mobilize publics and counterpublics through particular forms of gendered belonging and affective worldmaking.

The third line of inquiry theorizes our critical engagement with narratives of gendered belonging. Given readers' specific positionalities, what are the potentials and limitations of narratives and their reception for affective relating, identification, and societal and political transformation? Conceiving of storytelling as expressions of one's identity, as Shafak does, might also mean that we mistake narrative portrayals for lived realities. How might we conceptualize narrative counterpublics reparatively, i.e., through reparative methodologies founded in a common vision of recovering the lives and narratives of marginalized individuals and honoring their collective strategies of resistance and survival, without assuming such a reductive mimetic relationship? According to Eve Kosofsky Sedgwick, with regards to cultural and literary encounters, a reparative practice is characterized by the willingness "to experience surprise," both "terrible" and "good" (*Touching* 146), as it strives to discover "the many ways selves and communities succeed in extracting sustenance from the object of a culture—even of a culture whose avowed desire has often been not to sustain them" (*Touching* 150–151). To achieve this, the reparative reader "seek[s] new environments of sensation for the objects they study by displacing critical attachments once forged by correction, rejection, and anger with those crafted by affection, gratitude, solidarity, and love" (Wiegman, "Times" 7). In this sense, our project pays attention to the ambivalence that affective responses might contain and, ultimately, perhaps, the impossibility of grasping and unequivocally naming affect's effect.

Counteracting Marginalization: Affective Worldmaking as Counterpublic Strategies

Notions of worldmaking have long been in circulation in literary and cultural studies, but with the recent turns to affect, they have begun to re-shape ideas about the affective potential of narratives, well beyond post-classical narratology and reader response theory.[1] Our notion of affective worldmaking attends to the ways in which particular affects become tangible in narratives in different media and how they potentially inflect audiences' outlook on the world, especially with regard to prevalent notions of gender and sexuality. This emphasis on the affective dimensions not only conceives of the reader as an implied instance but also as a sentient being who may or may not share the texts' ethos and may or may not be literate in the cultural codes via which affect

---

1   For a discussion of worldmaking in media studies and narratology, see Bell and Ryan as well as V. Nünning, A. Nünning, and Neumann. See Goodman for a constructivist theorization of symbol systems and Zunshine for a neuroscientific one.

circulates. As prepersonal "intensity" (Massumi, *Parables* 24) and characterized by an "irreducibly bodily and autonomic nature" (Massumi, *Parables* 26), affect circulates via narratives. In turn, narratives can do a variety of cultural and political work, all centered around different affective responses: empathy, disgust, guilt, hope, and many more. Centering theorizations of literature's ability to do something to and with readers on texts' affective dimensions can generate novel insights into readers' ways of engaging with texts emotionally. Starting with observations about what Stephen Ahern has termed a "feel for the text" (1), and engaging with texts reparatively, throws into relief those intensities of being through which a sense of belonging can be manifested.[2]

Affect-centered scholarship has, by now, a robust tradition in literary studies. This ranges from neuroscientific work on reading to affect-based narratology.[3] Two of the most prominent traditions in literary studies today that investigate affect revolve around feminist and queer theorist work, on the one hand, and cognitive approaches to reading, on the other.[4] These diverging traditions employ affect-based understandings of the relationships between readers and texts to different ends. Especially from the perspective of feminist and queer narratology, affect plays a significant role in understanding narrative strategies such as narrative voice, the formation of the characters, the relation between the characters, etc., as well as the readers' affective attachments to narratives. Within the tradition of feminist and queer theorist work, Robyn Warhol's groundbreaking study, *Having a Good Cry: Effeminate Feelings and Pop-Culture Forms* (2003), observes that "[r]eading is a physical act" and recalls "the affects reading generates in our bodies" (ix). Warhol's project focuses on the somatic and sensory manifestations of reading experiences, including more immediate effects on readers' moods and more belated effects, such as laugh lines, on readers' faces.

---

2   For a discussion of the "reparative turn" in queer feminist critique, see Wiegman.

3   For more detailed discussions of these issues, see Ahern; Wehrs and Blake.

4   For an overview of recent queer and feminist narrative theory, see Warhol and Lanser; for an overview of cognitive literary studies, see Aldama.

Building on feminist and queer literary studies, Warhol theorizes the affective attachments that emerge between readers and texts via aesthetic experience. In contrast, neuroscientific work on literature's affective dimensions employs scientific conceptualizations of cognitive processes. Patrick Colm Hogan's seminal study, *Affective Narratology: The Emotional Structure of Stories* (2011), brings together work on narratological structures—primarily plot—with neuroscientific insights based on "biological factors" (7). Comparing Warhol and Colm Hogan's respective work indicates that, while they are both concerned with affective impressions, their fundamental understanding of readers differs considerably. While Colm Hogan's work assumes readers to be similarly programmed to decode texts' affective work, Warhol's work, in contrast, conceives of readers as particularly interpellated, due to their prior experiences, social status, and cognizance of literary conventions. Thus, Warhol's understanding of readers resonates more strongly with postmodern theories that define identities as being non-essentialist, performative, and relational.

Affect's relational properties are also at the center of notions of worldmaking derived from critical theory. While there are several different critical traditions of affect theory,[5] Gilles Deleuze and Felix

---

5   Gregg and Seigworth identify eight main orientations in affect studies by arranging them according to disciplines (6–8): 1. phenomenologies and post-phenomenologies of embodiment, 2. cybernetics and neurosciences focusing on the assemblages of human, machine, and the inorganic, 3. philosophy and philosophically inflected cultural studies linking matter with processual incorporeality, 4. psychological and psychoanalytic research combining biologism with broader systems of social desiring, 5. politically engaged work stemming from feminist, queer, disability and subaltern studies understanding individual experiences as collective, 6. research positioned between the linguistic turn's social constructionism and cognitive science, 7. critical inquiries of emotions beyond mere subjectivity, 8. science studies, especially focusing on materialism. See also Kate Stanley's discussion of different critical traditions in affect studies.

Guattari's work on assemblage[6] has been particularly instrumental to concepts of worldmaking which foreground the multidimensional processes and connections between authors, readers, and protagonists via the text. In her syncretic model of narrative worldmaking, Claudia Breger applies assemblage theory to "the rhetorical loops of composition (or production) and reading (or spectatorship)," in an attempt to understand the "performative process of configuring affects, associations, attention, experiences, evaluations, forms, matter, perspectives, perceptions, senses, sense, topoi and tropes in and through specific media, including mental operations as well as graphic notations, words and gestures, images and sounds" ("Narratology" 242).[7] To this end, Breger conceives of narratives as forms of affective configuration that emerge from the emotional, somatic, or visceral responses between readers, narrators, characters, and authors. The affective potential of texts and media is therefore actualized when readers "perform[] comparisons" and make "associations" between previous affective experiences and textual and social encounters and the narratives they consume, affectively "orienting" themselves in relation to them (Breger, "Narratology" 245). Breger's notion of "affect in configuration" applies simultaneously to the protagonists' affective storyworlds, the narrative's rhetorical strategies of evoking affective responses, and the readers' predisposition to engage with texts on an affective level. As far as readers' involvement in affective worldmaking is concerned, Breger contends that "they interweave heterogeneous pieces of their (actual or fantasy) worlds . . . into their reception of the (analogously composed) 'invented'" ("Affect" 236). Consequently, processes of affective worldmaking are marked by complex, spontaneous, and unpredictable associations between elements of stories and our "lifeworld experiences" (Breger, "Affect" 244) and their associated affects. As such, they hold the potential to *(re)configure* our relationships

---

6   The concept of assemblage runs through much of Deleuze and Guattri's work yet is never explicitly defined. For a typology of Deleuze and Guattari's assemblage theory, see Nail.

7   See also Claudia Breger's chapter in this volume.

not only to the respective narrative but also to ourselves, our lives, and others.

Among the many responses that narratives may prompt is also a sense of hope. Narratives can invite readers into alternative worlds in which their own identities are affirmed, accepted, and appreciated. This kind of affective worldmaking validates readers' experiences in ways that they have yet to see in the real world. For instance, non-essentialist narratives about LGBTQIA+ folks may act "as lifelines for those deprived of other forms of public acknowledgment" in the face of the "patent asymmetry and unevenness of structures of recognition" (Felski, *Uses* 43). Indeed, as José Esteban Muñoz asserts in *Cruising Utopia: The Then and There of Queer Futurity* (2009), the heteronormative and cisnormative present can be made more bearable if it is "known in relation to the alternative temporal and spatial maps provided by a perception of past and future affective worlds" (*Cruising* 27). Narratives then become part of an "archive of feelings" (Cvetkovich), which honors minoritized and marginalized communities by validating their experiences through the dissemination of their narratives. Heather K. Love's insightful study, *Feeling Backward: Loss and the Politics of Queer History* (2007), demonstrates that "feelings such as nostalgia, regret, shame, despair, ressentiment, passivity, escapism, self-hatred, withdrawal, bitterness, defeatism, and loneliness . . . are tied to the experience of social exclusion and to the historical 'impossibility' of same-sex desire" (4). While the historical discourses surrounding sexual stigmatization cannot be undone, rendering them visible and writing back at them may reclaim agency in the face of present-day discrimination and hostility. This affective worldmaking centers on the kinds of queer potentialities most forcefully described by Muñoz: "Queerness is essentially about the rejection of a here and now and an insistence on potentiality for another world" (*Cruising* 1).

Therefore, practices of affective worldmaking also engender counterpublics whose sense of affiliation coheres around shared experiences of oppression, marginalization, and discrimination. Narratives themselves may hold potentialities for alternative worlds, and the circulation of these narratives provides further ground for communities to emerge. Affective worldmaking's relational and multi-vectoral dynamics thus also generate a sense of community among readers. This notion of worldmaking builds on queer and feminist work on the public sphere. Additionally, work on the political salience of the personal and theorizations of the dialectical relationship between the public and the private has generated a new appreciation for the worldmaking potentialities of narratives.[8] Scholars such as Muñoz, Michael Warner, Nancy Fraser, and Rita Felski—in reverse chronological order—have introduced definitions of counterpublics that emphasize texts' agential function in the creation of counter-hegemonic communities through discursive practices and embodied activism. For instance, Warner defines counterpublics as "a multicontextual space of circulation, organized not by a place or an institution but by the circulation of discourse" (85) and as "a scene in which a dominated group aspires to re-create itself as a public and, in doing so, finds itself in conflict not only with the dominant social group, but also with the norms that constitute the dominant culture as a public" (80). In theorizing counterpublics, Warner and Muñoz foreground rhetoric, discourse, and representation in their discussions of the dissemination of books and the emergence of performance culture.[9] In turn, Nancy Fraser, whose work they reference, evokes the importance of communal spaces that facilitate collective engagement in a shared political project. Fraser's concept of "feminist subaltern counterpublics" depends on "subaltern counterpublics in order to signal that they are parallel discursive arenas where members of subordinated social groups invent and circulate counterdiscourses, which in turn permit them to formulate oppositional interpretations of their identities, interests, and needs" (67). For Fraser, these spaces are spaces of knowledge production: "variegated array of journals, bookstores, publishing companies, film and video distribution networks, lec-

---

8   The feminist credo that the personal is political comes to mind here and, in the specific context of American studies, the research collective "No More Separate Spheres!" (see Davidson).

9   Warner also speaks about concrete spaces like gay bars, sex shops, etc. See Berlant and Warner, "Sex in Public."

ture series, research centers, academic programs, conferences, conventions, festivals, and local meeting places" (67). Like Warner and Muñoz, Fraser suggests that counterpublics form in relation and reaction to dominant publics. The narratives through which they do so operate on two levels: they affirm the shared ethos of members of oppressed communities, and they disrupt oppressive discourses that target them in the first place. As Rita Felski, who first introduced the notion of a "feminist counter-public" (155) in *Beyond Feminist Aesthetics: Feminist Literature and Social Change* (1989), holds: "The feminist public sphere, in other words, serves a dual function: internally, it generates a gender-specific identity grounded in a consciousness of community and solidarity among women; externally, it seeks to convince society as a whole of the validity of feminist claims, challenging existing structures of authority through political activity and theoretical critique" (168). As these discussions of feminist and queer counterpublics and their interrelation to affect studies were fundamentally grounded in questions of gender and sexuality, we will briefly trace their connections in the subsequent section.

The Personal is Political: Gender, Sexuality, and the Genealogy of Affect Studies

The so-called affective turn in the 1990s developed out of a critical confrontation with the poststructuralist emphasis on discourse and de-/construction and the accompanying disregard of materiality.[10] As part of this new materialist approach, the body and, therefore, affects, as bodily phenomena, received more attention, challenging prevalent poststructuralist inquiry. In their invigorating introduction to *The Affect Theory Reader* (2010), the first anthology of its kind, Melissa Gregg and Gregory J. Seigworth state that it would be impossible to distill existing research on affect into a single definition. Instead,

---

10   The anthology *Affekt und Geschlecht* (2014, Affect and Gender), which includes some of the most important texts in affect theory in German translation, is of particular interest for the German-speaking audience.

they highlight—much in the fashion of Roland Barthes' work—the multifaceted mosaic of affect theory by speaking of an "inventory of shimmers" (Gregg and Seigworth 11).

Nonetheless, they trace affect theory's emergence in the anglophone context by introducing Eve Kosofsky Sedgwick's and Adam Frank's essay, "Shame in the Cybernetic Fold," as well as Brian Massumi's "The Autonomy of Affect," as starting points for further explorations in affect studies as we understand them today. Published in 1995, these essays have shaped two dominant directions in affect studies: While Sedgwick and Frank rely on Silvan Tomkins's psychobiology of various affects (1962), Massumi refers to Gilles Deleuze's take on Baruch de Spinoza's philosophy of embodied experience (1988). Gregg and Seigworth summarize: "affect as the prime 'interest' motivator that comes to put the drive in bodily drives (Tomkins); affect as an entire, vital, and modulating field of myriad becomings across human and nonhuman (Deleuze)" (6). While Tomkins conceives of affects as innate motivators for human beings in establishing a relationship to their surroundings, Massumi differentiates between affects as autonomous bodily reactions, on the one hand, and emotions as conscious states of being, on the other.

Although early works in affect studies were preoccupied with distinguishing the concept of affect from its apparent synonyms like emotion, feeling, and sentiment, recent scholarship has focused on accounting for their correlations and interdependence as well as their importance for political mobilization, community building, and identity creation. Although Massumi and some other theorists strictly distinguish affects from emotions or feelings,[11] Marta Figlerowicz argues, "it is debatable whether these three experiences are really distinct, whether they can be experienced independently of each other, and which of them is 'truest'" (5). Likewise, Sara Ahmed asserts that, although it may be possible to

---

11   For a discussion of the difference between affect (as an unconscious reaction of the body to external stimuli) and emotion (as a conscious state of feeling or conventional/coded expression of affect in gestures and language), see Massumi, *Parables* 232 and Gould 26. For a distinction between affects and feelings, see Massumi, *Parables* 27 and Zournazi 5.

theoretically "separate an affective response from an [associated] emotion," this does not mean that they "are separate" in "everyday life." Rather, Ahmed asserts that "they are contiguous; they slide into each other; they stick, and cohere, even when they are separated" ("Creating" 32). Accordingly, in her book *The Cultural Politics of Emotion* (2004), Ahmed does not define what emotions are but looks at their impact instead. Understanding emotions as social and cultural practices, which define the self's relationship to others (subjects and objects), Ahmed calls attention to their role in the formation of surfaces or boundaries that provoke either inclusion or exclusion, thereby proving emotion's public dimension.

Acknowledging the interpenetration and resonance of affect theory's starting points, Gregg and Seigworth arrange the main orientations in affect studies according to disciplines. They argue that politically engaged work in affect studies has its origin in the ways in which feminist, queer, disability, and subaltern studies understand individual experiences to be collective, "where persistent, repetitious practices of power can simultaneously provide a body (or, better, collective bodies) with predicaments and potentials for realizing a world that subsists within and exceeds the horizons and boundaries of the norm" (Gregg and Seigworth 7). Especially Cvetkovich calls attention to the feminist roots of understanding the seemingly personal as being political, which allows us to revisit the genealogy of affect studies through a focus on gender and sexuality in this book.

In the 2003 special issue on Public Sentiments of *The Scholar and Feminist Online*, affect scholars Ann Cvetkovich and Ann Pellegrini question whether feelings, emotions, and affects—as conventionally assumed—are phenomena that can only be assigned to the private realm and the intimacy of kinship, partnership, and friendship. They convincingly show how the above-mentioned phenomena play a central role in the organization of public life as so-called public sentiments: "from the deployment of affect to produce national patriotism, to the rallying of audiences on behalf of social forms of oppression and violence, to passionate calls for activism" (ibid.). Speaking of "public feelings" later in their text, Cvetkovich and Pellegrini reveal that they strategically chose an often negatively connotated term for their special issue's title, namely "sentiment," that "[]bears the trace of that most disparaged of affective cultural forms, the 'sentimental', a term which continues to imply that particular feelings are excessive, insincere, and best relegated to the private. In other words: 'feminine'. . . . However, as feminist scholarship has also shown, sentimentality has been used to draw attention to important social issues" (ibid.). Similarly, Gregg Hendler's monograph, *Public Sentiments: Structures of Feeling in Nineteenth-Century American Literature* (2001), proposes that "feeling publicly" (11) is an affective experience in response to sentimental novels and their capacity not only to move readers privately but also to move them towards taking public action. Indeed, both Cvetkovich and Pellegrini's work and Hendler's text suggest that affect is public and political.

These connections between affect and the public sphere also found their expression in queer-feminist work on intimacy. In their book *The Queen of America Goes to Washington City* (1997), Lauren Berlant uses the example of the conservative Reagan era in US politics of the 1980s to illustrate what they coined the intimate public sphere: in public, the political manifests itself through the personal and the intimate: e.g., through campaigns against abortion, strengthening the traditional heteronormative family. According to Berlant, "institutions of intimacy" (Berlant, "Intimacy" 281) determine which narratives are privileged and thus worth striving for. Intimacies that go beyond the hegemonic conception of the heteronormative relationship between two people, privileged as a "life narrative" (Berlant, "Intimacy" 285), have not had an alternative canon, legal anchoring, or cultural manifestations so far. Thus, Berlant questions whether they are sustainable over longer periods of time. Problematizing the relationship between the hegemonic narrative of intimacy and its deviations in the delightfully titled article "Sex in Public," Berlant and Warner jointly formulate their concept of counterintimacies (562). The prerequisite for the formulation of counterintimacies is critical practical knowledge that allows them to be understood not only as transgressions from the norm or trivialized as a lifestyle but simply to be recognized as intimate. In the case of queer counterintimacies, this should not result in a simplified emphasis on the personal life plans of gays and lesbians. Rather, the complex affective, erotic, and personal aspects of counterintimacies should be understood as public—"public in the sense of accessible, available to memory, and sustained through collective activity" (ibid.).

In *The Female Complaint* (2008), Berlant further differentiates their idea of a public permeated by intimacy by discussing women's culture as one of numerous intimate publics (5). In doing so, they no longer focus only on the political content of women's culture, but also on its economic structure. Accordingly, an intimate public arises when a market opens up to selected consumers and claims to be circulating texts and goods that are of particular interest to them (ibid.). Intimate publics function—like the nations defined by Benedict Anderson (6) as imagined communities—through a feeling of belonging among strangers, which they believe existed before the establishment of a market that addresses them.[12] Berlant describes such publics, in the sense of Nancy Fraser, as "weak publics" (75), which are interested in the cultural upswing of certain groups but which do not necessarily address their structural disadvantage akin to strong publics (ibid.). Here, Berlant distances themself from the political concept of the counterpublic, which Warner formulates with recourse to Fraser: "Most nondominant collective public activity is not as saturated by the taxonomies of the political sphere as the counterpublic concept would suggest" (Berlant, *Female* 8). According to Berlant, in intimate public spheres, the political sphere is often perceived as a threat which degrades and retraumatizes rather than offering opportunities for transformation. Following Berlant's careful differentiation, we will discuss the potentials and limitations of affective worldmaking in the next section.

---

12   While Anderson focuses on the role of print capitalism and the use of common, increasingly standardized languages that create an image of the national community as being natural and long-standing (Anderson 46–47), Berlant looks at the more differentiated, modern mass-consumer market that targets specific social groups by referencing common-sense notions of conventional lifeworlds and experiences of such groups (Berlant, *Female* 5).

Beyond Empathy and Identification: Potentials and Limitations of Affective Worldmaking

Narratives are particularly conducive to affective worldmaking. Their use of plot development and character perspectives invites readers into the emotional storyworlds of novels, short stories, auto/biographical pieces, narrative poetry, newspaper articles, myths, and narrative films. They present situations where readers can witness the circulation of affect in moments of personal encounters among lovers, friends, family members, strangers, and allies. This focus on ontological and psychological dimensions of characters invites readers to partake in the sharing of feelings. As mentioned above, to think of narratives as opportunities to engage with the emotional worlds of characters and narrators is a well-established practice within various traditions of literary studies concerned with the workings of affect.

This is also the gist of Shafak's gripping statement about the power of stories to "bring us together" (9). Who is the "us" in her aphorism, one might ask, and what qualities of "togetherness" does she evoke? As her anecdote exemplifies, Shafak's own narrative takes precedence over the trans woman's story, which is vital for Shafak's story and acknowledged as important, but actually never gets told. In other words, this woman is a figure in Shafak's narrative but does not possess narrative agency herself. Given the untold nature of this woman's story, what does this mean for the potential emergence of a sense of solidarity, affinity, or kinship within Shafak's narration? Therefore, Shafak's example also seems to suggest that there are limits to the sense of belonging which affective worldmaking may generate.

Reading is not a zero-sum game: While readers may respond with a sense of sympathetic identification, affect may also register utterly ambivalently. A mimetic stance towards a text's affective dimensions oversimplifies affect's much more complex workings. For one, affect also circulates outside the realm of emotional responses to characters or narrators. Moreover, non-narrative texts also operate with affective economies that do not depend on depictions of lived experience, thoughts, or feelings. In *Affect and American Literature in the Age of Neoliberalism* (2015), Rachel Greenwald Smith argues that the "belief that literature is at its most meaningful when it represents and transmits the emotional specificity of personal experience" (1) extends neoliberalism's emphasis on the private and the individual into the realm of aesthetic reception, where readers "consume" (29) texts or emotionally "invest" (3) in the lives of the characters. Such affective attachments—which Greenwald Smith terms the "affective hypothesis" (1)—assume that feelings translate from the realm of the text into the realm of the audience.

Likewise, the theory that literary reading positively impacts readers' ethical and moral values is an appealing but perhaps ultimately not sustainable thought. The well-known empathy-altruism debate in literary studies is a great case in point. Popularized by philosopher Martha C. Nussbaum, the thought that novels provide readers an occasion to see and experience the world through someone else's eyes has gained significant traction. In her book *Poetic Justice: The Literary Imagination and Public Life* (1997), Nussbaum argues that novels are characterized by

> a commitment to the separateness of persons and to the irreducibility of quality to quantity; its sense that what happens to individuals in the world has enormous importance; its commitment to describe the events of life not from an external perspective of detachment, as the doings and movings of ants and machine parts, but from within, as invested with the complex significances with which human beings invest their own lives. (32)

However, Nussbaum's claim about novels' ability to shape readers' sense of justice overlooks the complex interrelationships between readers, characters, narrators, and texts. For instance, her focus on realist novels leads to assumptions that do not hold for experimental novels or novels about unfamiliar worlds and lives. Missing from Nussbaum's considerations are also the potential preconceptions readers may bring to texts and their unforeseeable aesthetic and emotional responses. Certainly, the utilitarian understanding of literature's valence, which Nussbaum employs, has been challenged by more recent work on aesthetics,[13] but the belief that literary reading can make us better people still holds strong to this day, possibly also due to the need to justify literary studies' worth in an era when neoliberalism increasingly shapes higher education.[14]

A more nuanced discussion of the relationship between reading and altruism has emerged from the scholarship of Suzanne Keen, who not only shares Nussbaum's interest in the novel's ability to create an empathetic response in its readers but also highlights the crucial role that readers play in this process. In her seminal study *Empathy and the Novel* and subsequent projects, Keen suggests that processes of "narrative empathy cannot be expected invariably to work," as readers' responses will vary (Keen, *Empathy* 72). According to Keen, "no one narrative text evokes empathy from all its readers" (Keen, "Readers' Temperament" 296). She argues that this is dependent on the respective "readers' cultural contexts and individual experiences," as these "influence the degree of their responsiveness to the emotional appeal of texts" (Keen, "Readers' Temperament" 296–297) and their resultant "collaboration in fictional worldmaking" (Keen, "Intersectional" 142). Moreover, although Keen maintains that processes of "narrative empathy" may allow readers to share the "feeling[s] and perspective[s]" of others and to empathize with their "situation and condition," she also holds that this rarely results in solidarity with members of represented minorities (Keen, "Narrative"). Indeed, even if readers "experience narrative empathy," this does not necessarily cause them to take "prosocial action in the real" (Keen, "Readers' Temperament" 297). Nonetheless, Keen still holds that "[n]arratives are extraordinarily effective devices for opening the channel of fellow feeling and breaking through barriers of difference thrown up by distance, time, culture, experience" ("Intersectional" 142).

---

13   See, among others, Sianne Ngai's *Ugly Feelings* and Jacques Rancière's "The Aesthetic Revolution."

14   Rita Felski's work on literature's "uses" openly addresses the necessity to legitimize literary studies by highlighting its benefits. Her *Uses of Literature* is a case in point.

While Nussbaum and Keen—as well as the critical traditions they have shaped—approach the novel's overall potential to generate empathy in different ways, they both center their studies around a shared premise: namely, that literary reading means engaging with the lives of others, the lives of fictional or historical persons. Both critics assume that the lives and worlds of these persons are different from those of readers and that readers may thereby encounter perspectives different from their own or from those of the people with whom they interact in "real life." In other words, literary reading may introduce us to new and unfamiliar ways of seeing and knowing the world.

Affect's inherent ambivalence can generate a variety of responses from readers. *Affective Worldmaking* shifts the focus towards a different dimension of interaction between texts and audiences, such as narratives' capacity to prompt or contribute to the emergence of counterpublics. By focusing on literature's function as "'windows' into [a] presumed alterity" (Amireh and Majaj, 2), critics like Nussbaum and Keen overlook the affirmative potential literature can have for readers who can relate to the struggles depicted in texts. For example, alterity and empathy for the other is less an issue when readers experience a sense of validation of their own queer identities through the engagement with narratives about queer lives. Similarly, recovering racial histories that are often overlooked or misconstrued in mainstream historiographies can offer points of recognition for racialized communities. In the same light, amidst prevalent ethno-nationalist myths of belonging, subversive narratives can affirm alternative registers, structures, and practices of community building.

Recognition can therefore occur on (at least) two levels: it can be a moment of recognizing one's (marginalized) identity in a text; it can also be a moment of recognizing one's affective responses to a text. With regards to the first one, Sarah Nuttall, for instance, argues, "[r]eading may often be about recognizing the self as known, identifiable or acknowledged by a text, as if for the first time" (391). For, as Rita Felski highlights, recognition in reading and representation can bring about both a "moment of personal illumination and heightened self-understanding" and "practices of acknowledgment," as well as "acceptance and validation," in the wider social and political realm (*Uses* 30). Surely, seeing one's experiences acknowledged within narratives of various media may help to mitigate feelings of isolation and invalidation. In fact, as Hil Malatino argues with regards to transgender rage, moments of recognition may help process trauma and (re-)build resilience through witnessing that others also "share a similar crucible" (Malatino, "Though" 135). This can produce a sense of communality that seems to emanate from a shared feeling of "history" between readers, texts, characters, narrators, and authors and "their ongoing attachments and actions" (Berlant, *Female* 5). Similarly, Felski notes that reading as an "[a]esthetic experience crystallizes an awareness of forming part of a broader community." Consequently, moments of recognition in textual or interpersonal encounters "may offer solace and relief not to be found elsewhere, confirming that I am not entirely alone, that there are others who think or feel like me" (Felski, *Uses* 33). Indeed, Lauren Berlant suggests that "a tiny point of identification can open up a field of fantasy and de-isolation, of vague continuity, or of ambivalence" (Berlant, *Female* 11). Moreover, as Silvia Schultermandl suggests, readers may also "feel[] connected to an unknown reading public based on the understanding that what unites them is their experience of the affective structures a text evokes" (253), as they "become part of the text" by "invest[ing]" their "own ideas[,]" experiences, and emotions "into the text" (260).

On the other hand, members of marginalized communities are also able to engage in resistant worldmaking practices through narratives that fail to address them. To this end, Muñoz introduces the notion of "disidentification" to highlight how minoritarian communities engage in worldmaking practices by de- and reconstructing majoritarian culture to establish "alternate views of the world" (*Disidentification* 195–196). According to Muñoz, "[t]o disidentify is to read oneself and one's own life narrative in a moment, object, or subject that is not culturally coded to 'connect' with the disidentifying subject" (*Disidentification* 12). Yet, as Muñoz makes clear, these strategies of narrative production and reception (*Disidentification* 72) are neither wholehearted rejections of dominant discourse nor their reproductions, but rather "both expose[] the encoded message's universalizing and exclusionary machinations and recircuit[] its workings to account for, include, and empower minority identities and identifications" (*Disidentification* 31). However, moments of recognition may not only be reassuring or empowering. They can also be marked by experiences of discomfort and disruption and may even be (re-)traumatizing. As Rita Felski suggests, "moments of self-apprehension can trigger a spectrum of emotional reactions shading from delight to discomfort, from joy to chagrin" (Felski, *Uses* 29). In fact, Suzanne Keen argues that "[e]xtreme personal distress in response to narrative usually interrupts and sometimes terminates the narrative transaction" and with it affective worldmaking (Keen, "Narrative").

Recognition, however, does not only mean seeing one's identity represented in and therefore acknowledged by a narrative, but it is also a worldmaking endeavor in the sense that it asks readers to engage with and interrogate their own identities and experiences. In *Uses of Literature* (2008), Rita Felski names recognition as one particular aesthetic experience through which readers might relate to texts. Distinguishing recognition from the more unilateral practice of identification, Felski suggests that "[w]hen we recognize something, we literally 'know it again'; we make sense of what is unfamiliar by fitting it into an existing scheme, linking it to what we already know" (*Uses* 25). This etymological precision of the term 'recognition' as re-knowing something rather than identifying with something previously unknown highlights the "metaphorical and self-reflexive dimensions of literary representation" (Uses 44) and leads Felski to conclude that "[w]e do not glimpse aspects of ourselves in literary works because these works are repositories for unchanging truths about the human condition ... Rather, any flash of recognition arises from an interplay between texts and the fluctuating beliefs, hopes, and fears of readers" (*Uses* 46). Like Felski, Winfried Fluck describes recognition as a dynamic worldmaking process. Fluck terms recognition as the "in-between state" (58) readers must occupy, in order to actualize the protagonist in the fictional world they have never experienced themselves. Readers do so by drawing from their personal experiences of the world around them and bringing their own views to the text. In this vein, literary reading is an exercise not primarily in getting to know a new world but in getting to know oneself, prompted by the aesthetic experience with a literary text. Furthermore, the ways in which readers may come to feel a text will depend on the experiences and connections they draw on and not just the texts themselves (Steinbock, 10). For, as Sara Ahmed reminds us in *The Promise of Happiness* (2010), "what we may feel depends on the angle of our arrival" (41) as well as the contents of a given situation or text. In other words, potential moments of affirmation and recognition are actualized differently, depending on the respective reader's intersectional positionality and the content of the respective narrative. This, in turn, also implies that a text's potential for evoking recognition and affective interpellation is not universal, guaranteed, or necessarily unproblematic. In fact, as Fraser makes clear, despite their potential for "expand[ing] discursive space[s,]" subaltern counterpublics can also be marked by "their own modes of informal exclusion and marginalization" (Fraser 67).

Moreover, Felski emphasizes that a purely reductionist reading or interpretation of texts reproduces a "naïve realism" (Felski, *Beyond* 79) which runs the risk of reducing the text purely to its political function. According to Felski, a "repoliticization of culture" (Felski, *Beyond* 167) helps to re-embed texts and their reception within broader social contexts. It highlights the dialectics of politics and aesthetics rather than neglecting one in favor of the other in a one-dimensional reading. Hence, studying the political implications of texts should not be equated with reading them as a straightforward instrument of ideology.

The study of affective worldmaking can help clarify the relationships between the aesthetic dimensions of texts and the socio-political worlds inhabited by their readers, thus giving insight into potentials for the formation and perseverance of identity and community as well as for political action via textual encounters or through inspiration from the text. By combining theoretical, literary, and analytical texts, our edited volume hopes to offer methodological impulses and reflect on the possibilities and limitations of combining affect with literary, cultural, and media studies.

Structure of the book

The structure of this edited volume reflects our engagement with various genres, media forms, and functions of affective worldmaking that we understand as the entanglement of narrative and affective structures. The contributions not only discuss but also represent and illustrate these different functions. The volume combines theoretical reflections on narrative, affect, the creation of publics—in short, the interwoven aspects we understand as affective worldmaking—and analyses of concrete examples from various media forms and various geopolitical and cultural contexts, with examples of literary and artistic practices that are consciously engaged in the project of worldmaking. In this way, the volume brings into conversation academic practices of theoretical reflection (from literary and film studies to media and discourse analysis) with artistic and activist practices concerned with challenging social norms and narratives and the creation of new social relations, affective structures, and publics.

Consequently, the book offers foundational theoretical texts and examples of academic analyses and connects these to the field of political organizing and social movements, while continuously reflecting on the interconnections of the different 'publics' or discursive and practical platforms and their differences. The transnational scope of the volume aims to detach the theoretical models discussed above from their narrow cultural and political contexts—a narrowness that frequently remains unacknowledged, suggesting an illusionary universal validity of theories originating from North America or Western Europe. The volume attempts to test the applicability of theories and concepts of affect and narrative to different spatial and temporal contexts as well as to assorted media forms. The contributions critically engage in theoretical canons of gender and affect studies and illuminate parallels and specificities to enhance a better understanding of theories of affect, gender, and sexuality, in addition to their associated analytical and methodological practices.

The question of media form and genre is not only reflected in the book's structure but is also directly discussed in the individual essays.

Using the study of narrative and storytelling as a connecting analytical mode, the contributions examine a variety of texts (in the wider sense of the word, including film, artworks, and performance) and thus bring together various fields of media and literary analysis. The contributions tackle the question of how form and content relate in different media, how narrative strategies relate to affective responses, empathy, recognition, and identification, and how the media form impacts the mode of circulation and communicative practices associated with the production and consumption of narratives.

The book's contributions are arranged in three separate parts concerned with different aspects and functions of affective worldmaking. They are enclosed by two contemporary artistic texts: the collection opens with a selection of poems by Adisa Bašić, which appear here for the first time in English translation by Mirza Purić. These poems focus on the gendered experiences of women in Bosnian-Herzegovinian post-war society. The edited collection closes with the chapter "Plan B" from the graphic novel *Zemlja–voda–zrak* (2020, Earth–Water–Air, translated by Tag McEntegart), edited by Damir Arsenijević, written by Šejla Šehabović, and illustrated by Marko Gačnik. It is part of a newly established platform of the same name, which promotes environmental humanities in Bosnia-Herzegovina at the intersection of activism, academia, and art. With these creative pieces bookending our edited collection, we aim to combine the affective experience of texts with the theoretical reflection on affect and reading offered in the book.

The first part, "Senses of Affective Worldmaking," lays out the main theoretical observations that have informed our collaborative work and the development of our concept of affective worldmaking. It uses different genres of text to highlight the multiplicity of possible approaches to this field of study. Claudia Breger's essay connects her theory of narrative worldmaking with the Deleuzian concept of affective assemblages, underlining the connections of narrative and affect, their worldbuilding properties, and the potentials and limitations of the idea of reparative reading. May Friedman makes use of the personal reflective essay to disentangle the interconnections of larger affective narratives and structures and the navigation of one's own personal life and academic practices along (or against) those normative structures. Deborah D.E.E.P. Mouton's short essay exemplifies how black writers reclaim agency through writing mythology, thereby demonstrating the importance of counternarratives and histories for those excluded from dominant narratives, worldmaking practices, and publics. Lastly, a conversation with Ann Cvetkovich draws from her extensive theoretical work in affect studies and reflects on the various levels of academic, artistic, and activist practices and how these practices can help in understanding the complex interrelations between the political and the personal in public spheres and the way affective structures connect, separate, and shape them.

The second part, "Affective Be/Longing: Redefining Public Spheres," discusses the 'public sphere' as a discursive and communicative reality as well as a theoretical concept to analyze communicative structures and the circulation of norms, ideas, and values in societies. The contributions critically engage with the concept of the public: What constitutes a public or multiple publics, whose voices are heard or silenced, which rules and structures govern communication, discourse, and the reception and reproduction of discursive patterns? They ask what enables people to access dominant discourses and affective structures—i.e., what makes people feel they 'belong' or feel seen, heard, or represented within various public platforms. Si Sophie Pages Whybrew's contribution analyzes the worldmaking potential of North American science fiction stories for trans readers, reflecting on the relationship of a particular genre to a specific audience and its implications for representation and recognition. Jelena Petrović traces continuities of Marxist feminist theories of emotional and reproductive labor in contemporary art and performance in the post-Yugoslav space against the backdrop of a revisionist conservative turn. In a conversation about their graphic novel *Zemlja−voda−zrak* (Earth−Water−Air), Damir Arsenijević and Šejla Šehabović discuss 'public feelings' in response to Bosnia-Herzegovina's transition from socialism to capitalism and their complex linkages to questions of social and environmental justice. Jana Aresin outlines the way women's magazines in the immediate post-WWII period in Japan used different narrative and affective strategies to renegotiate identities of womanhood and femininity in the face of the disruption and delegitimization of previously dominant narratives and ideals. Heike Paul's contribution reflects on the way the motif of family separation has been used in US literature in different time periods and contexts to elicit sympathy and identification, while questioning in how far this narrative strategy challenges or reaffirms normative social relations.

The third part, "Counternarratives and Community Building," shifts the perspective from the side of the production of discourse and narratives and focuses more concretely on the reception of a multiplicity of publics. It investigates if and in what ways the emergence of different publics can potentially lead to the development of alternative communities and forms of resistance to dominant norms, ideals, and affective structures, while critically reflecting the notion of the counterpublic. The contributions focus on the political potential and limitation of alternative and marginalized forms of community building, of the role of counternarratives within society and the tension between representation and recognition within a hegemonic public sphere that is perceived as homogeneous and that exerts a normative force, and other (counter)publics that offer different forms of being, feeling, and belonging.

Dijana Simić discusses two examples of contemporary Bosnian-Herzegovinian fiction and their reparative potential by centering on otherwise overlooked lesbian narratives. Iveta Jansová analyses creative and participatory practices of queer media fans, in response to the absence of queer representation in mainstream media. Renate Hansen-Kokoruš's contribution is concerned with the political potential of satire and humor in challenging social norms, without alienating conservative readers. Silvia Schultermandl turns to the affective communities and new protest forms created in social media activism in response to sexual harassment and violence. Lastly, Ahmet Atay takes the COVID-19 pandemic as a starting point to reflect on the affective functions of fictional narratives and characters in times of social isolation.

Even though we have separated the contributions into different categories, based on their main focus, there is naturally an overlap between the different topics. All works reflect on both the production and reception side of narratives, how they are connected, and how affect circulates between them. And they all expand on theoretical considerations while referencing selected case studies and personal experiences.

As mentioned above, this collection aims to cover a wide geographical and temporal range but has, unsurprisingly, still left many blind spots. Nevertheless, we believe that the contributions will not only prove to be of interest to scholars of the specific regions covered here, but they also raise larger questions regarding the study of affect and the universality or limitations of foundational theoretical texts in affect studies by North American writers. We further attempted to cover a wide range of media, including literary texts of various genres, magazines, graphic novels, TV series, art exhibitions, archival projects, and social media content. As such, this book provides paradigmatic examples that are intended to serve as a starting point for the study of affective worldmaking in different media forms from a comparative perspective.

Lastly, while most of our contributions share a strong focus on analyzing factors of class, gender, and sexuality, other important identity categories that impact both the production and reception of affect in media, such as race, ethnicity, religion, age, and dis/ability, require further study in our future research. The goal of this collection is to examine the manifold ways different social groups and communities negotiate and fight for their place in society, how they define or question their own and others' identities and social norms and values through narratives in various media. It is concerned with the relation between storytelling and political and social agency—again referring to Shafak's essay, the dominant stories through which we negotiate our lived realities and identities as well as the untold and silenced stories that are yet to be uncovered and reclaimed.

Bibliography

Ahern, Stephen. "Introduction: A Feel for the Text." In *Affect Theory and Literary Critical Practice: A Feel for the Text*, edited by Stephen Ahern. Palgrave Macmillan, 2019, pp. 1–21.

Ahmed, Sara. *The Promise of Happiness*. Duke UP, 2010.

———. "Creating Disturbance: Feminism, Happiness and Affective Differences." In *Working with Affect in Feminist Readings: Disturbing Differences*, edited by Marianne Liljeström and Susanna Paasonen. Routledge, 2010, pp. 32–44.

Aldama, Frederick Luis, ed. *Towards a Cognitive Theory of Literary Acts*. U of Texas P, 2010.

Amireh, Amal, and Lisa Suhair Majaj. "Introduction." In *Going Global: The Transnational Reception of Third World Women Writers*, edited by Amal Amireh and Lisa Suhair Majaj. Garland, 2000, pp. 1–25.

Anderson, Benedict. *Imagined Communities: Reflections on the Origin and Spread of Nationalism*. Verso, 2006 [1983].

Arsenijević, Damir, Šejla Šehabović and Marko Gačnik. Zemlja–voda–zrak. Muzej književnosti i pozorišne umjetnosti Bosne i Hercegovine. 2020.

Baier, Angelika, Binswanger, Christa, Häberlein, Jana and Nay, Yv Eveline, eds. *Affekt und Geschlecht: Eine einführende Anthologie*. Zaglossus, 2014.

Bell, Alice, and Marie-Laure Ryan, eds. *Possible Worlds Theory and Contemporary Narratology*. U of Nebraska P, 2019.

Berlant, Lauren. "The Intimate Public Sphere." In: *Emotions. A Cultural Studies Reader*, edited by Jennifer Harding and E. Deidre Pribram. Routledge, 2009, 280–289.

———. *The Female Complaint: The Unfinished Business of Sentimentality in American Culture*. Duke UP, 2008.

———. *The Queen of America Goes to Washington City: Essays on Sex and Citizenship*. Durham, 1997.

———, ed. *Intimacy*. U of Chicago P, 2000.

———. "Intimacy: A Special Issue" *Critical Inquiry* vol.24, no. 2, 1998, pp. 281–288.

——, and Michael Warner. "Sex in Public." *Critical Inquiry*, vol. 24, no. 2, 1998, pp. 547–566.

Breger, Claudia. "Affects in Configuration: A New Approach to Narrative Worldmaking." *Narrative*, vol. 25, no. 2, 2017, pp. 227–51.

——. "Affect and Narratology." In *The Palgrave Handbook of Affect Studies and Textual Criticism*, edited by Ronald R. Wehrs and Thomas Blake, Palgrave Macmillan, 2017, 235–57.

Cvetkovich, Ann. *An Archive of Feelings: Trauma, Sexuality, and Lesbian Public Cultures*. Duke UP, 2003.

——. "Public Feelings." *South Atlantic Quarterly*, vol. 106, no. 3, 2007, pp. 459–468.

——, and Ann Pellegrini. (2003): "Introduction." In: The Scholar and Feminist Online (Public Sentiments) 2/1. sfonline.barnard.edu/ps/intro.htm [22.02.2020].

Davidson, Cathy N. "Preface: No More Separate Spheres!" *American Literature* special issue on No More Separate Spheres!, vol. 70., no. 3, 1998, pp. 443–63.

Felski, Rita. *Uses of Literature*. Blackwell, 2008.

——. *Beyond Feminist Aesthetics: Feminist Literature and Social Change*. Harvard UP, 1989.

Figlerowicz, Marta. "Affect Theory Dossier: An Introduction." *Qui Parle*, vol. 20, no. 2, 2012, pp. 3–18.

Fluck, Winfried. "Reading for Recognition." *New Literary History*, vol. 44, no.1, 2013, pp. 45–67.

Fraser, Nancy. "Rethinking the Public Sphere: A Contribution to the Critique of Actually Existing Democracy." *Social Text*, vol. 25/26, 1990, pp. 50–85.

Goodman, Nelson. *Ways of Worldmaking*. Harvard UP, 1978.

Gould, Deborah. "On Affect and Protest." In *Political Emotion: New Agendas in Communication*, edited by Janet Staiger, Ann Cvetkovich, and Ann Reynolds. Routledge, 2010, pp. 18–44.

Greenwald Smith, Rachel. *Affect and American Literature in the Age of Neoliberalism*. Cambridge UP, 2015.

Gregg, Melissa, and Gregory J. Seigworth, eds. *The Affect Theory Reader*. Duke UP, 2010.

Hendler, Gregg. *Public Sentiments: Structures of Feeling in Nineteenth-Century American Literature*. U of North Carolina P, 2011.

Hogan, Patrick Colm. *Affective Narratology: The Emotional Structure of Stories*. U of Nebraska P, 2011.

Keen, Suzanne. *Empathy and the Novel*. Oxford UP, 2010.

———. "Intersectional Narratology in the Study of Narrative Empathy." In *Narrative Theory Unbound: Queer and Feminist Interventions*, edited by Robyn R. Warhol and Susan S. Lanser. The Ohio State UP, 2015, pp. 123–24.

———. "Readers' Temperament and Fictional Character." *New Literary History*, vol.42, 2011, pp. 295–314.

———. "Narrative Empathy." *The Living Handbook of Narratology*, edited by Jan Christoph Meister et al., Hamburg University, 2013, http://www.lhn.uni-hamburg.de/node/42.html.

———. "Readers' Temperaments and Fictional Character." *New Literary History*, vol. 42, no. 2, 2011, pp. 295–314.

Love, Heather. *Feeling Backward: Loss and the Politics of Queer History*. Harvard UP, 2007.

Malatino, Hil. "Tough Breaks: Trans Rage and the Cultivation of Resilience." *Hypatia*, vol. 34, no. 1, 2019, pp. 121–40.

Massumi, Brian. "The Autonomy of Affect." *Culture Critique*, vol. 31, 1995, pp. 83–109.

———. *Parables for the Virtual. Movement, Affect, Sensation*. Duke UP, 2002.

Muñoz, José Esteban. *Cruising Utopia: The Then and There of Queer Futurity*. NYU P, 2009.

———. *Disidentifications: Queers of Color and the Performance of Politics*. U of Minnesota P, 1999.

Nail, Thomas. "What is an Assemblage?" *SubStance* vol. 46, no.1, 2017, pp. 21–37.

Ngai, Sianne. *Ugly Feelings*. Harvard UP, 2005.

Nünning, Vera, Nünning, Ansgar, and Birgit Neumann, eds. *Cultural Ways of Worldmaking: Media and Narratives*. De Gruyter, 2010.

Nussbaum, Martha C. *Poetic Justice: The Literary Imagination and Public Life*. Beacon P, 1997.

Nuttall, Sarah. "Reading, Recognition and the Postcolonial." *Interventions*, vol. 3, no. 3, Jan. 2001, pp. 391–404.

Rancière, Jacques. "The Aesthetic Revolution and its Outcomes: Emplotments of Autonomy and Heteronomy." *New Left Review*, vol. 14, Mar./Apr. 2002, pp. 133–151.

Schultermandl, Silvia. *Ambivalent Transnational Belonging in American Literature*. Routledge, 2021.

——. "Reading for Connectivity: Aesthetics and Affect in Intermedial Autobiographies 2.0." *Interactions: Studies in Communication & Culture*, vol. 9, no. 2, July 2018, pp. 251–63.

Sedgwick, Eve Kosofsky. *Touching Feeling: Affect, Pedagogy, Performativity*. Duke UP, 2003.

——, and Adam Frank. "Shame in the Cybernetic Fold: Reading Silvan Tomkins." *Critical Inquiry*, vol. 21, no. 2, Winter 1995, pp. 496–522.

Shafak, Elif. *How to Stay Sane in An Age of Division*. Profile Books, 2020.

Staiger, Janet, Cvetkovich, Ann, and Ann Reynolds. "Introduction: Political Emotions and Public Feelings." In: *Political Emotions: New Agendas in Communication*, edited by Janet, Staiger, Ann, Cvetkovich, and Ann Reynolds. Routledge, 2010, pp. 1–17.

Stanely, Kate. "Affect and Emotion: James, Dewey, Tomkins, Damasio, Massumi, Spinoza." In *The Palgrave Handbook of Affect Studies and Textual Criticism*, edited by Ronald R. Wehrs and Thomas Blake. Palgrave Macmillan, 2017, pp. 97–112.

Stewart, Kathleen. *Ordinary Affects*. Duke UP, 2007.

Warhol, Robyn. *Having a Good Cry: Effeminate Feelings and Pop-Culture Forms*. Ohio State UP, 2003.

——, and Susan S. Lanser, eds. *Narrative Theory Unbound: Queer and Feminist Interventions*. Ohio State UP, 2015.

Warner, Michael. "Publics and Counterpublics." *Public Culture*, vol. 14, no. 1, 2002, pp. 49–90.

Wehrs, Donald R. and Thomas Blake, eds. *The Palgrave Handbook of Affect Studies and Textual Criticism*. Palgrave Macmillan, 2017.

Wiegman, Robyn. "The Times We're In: Queer Feminist Criticism and the Reparative 'Turn.'" *Feminist Theory*, vol. 15, no.1, 2014, pp. 4–25.

Zournazi, Mary. "Navigating Movements." In *Politics of Affect*, edited by Brian Massumi. Polity, 2015, pp. 1–46.

Zunshine, Lisa. *Why We Read Fiction: Theory of Mind and the Novel*. Ohio State UP, 2006.

Selected Poems

Adisa Bašić (Translated by Mirza Purić)

I SPEAK

It's not just *my* scarred face, *my* riven soul,
    my tormented body.

I also speak for three lepers
    one who is filthy
    four who are pitiable
    a thousand mutes
    two with a club foot
    ten who've never had a man
    five thousand cloistered ones
    and four whose heads are covered.

For three who are denied a job
    two who don't go to school for they *aren't whores*
    three hundred who've been raped for they *are whores*.

For a little one
    who believes she's leprous filthy pitiable mute.

And for one who is free
    who meekly waits
    to be born.

TAMENESS

You love me mindlessly precisely because I'm *mad*.
    I perform stunts in bed.
    I cook naked.
    I press the citrus squeezer on my mouth
    and talk like Darth Vader
    and you laugh.

When I smuggle bits of my madness outside
    in my hair, my bra, or under my tongue —
    that makes you sick.

Beyond our four walls
    even laughing out loud
    is quite, quite inappropriate.

HEROINE

He's gone and gone and gone.
    His smell evanesced from the clothes in the wardrobe.
    Kids think they remember him.

Long hath he lain here before thee
    And after thee
    Long shall he lie ...

Underneath a virgin patch of grass.
    Underneath a layer of leaves.

He's gone and gone and gone.
    And you wake over a shriveled memory.
    His likeness: a pressed flower.

Profusely we praise your dignity.
    You're the love we dream of.
    You're the loyalty we wish for.
    You're the picture that fits our frame.

And he's gone.
    And gone.
    And gone.

Nobody hears the night.
    You bite your hands till you bleed.
    Put fingers into yourself.
    Bang your head on the headboard.

In your lonely bed, you know:
    you don't remember him.

DOMINATION

the well-groomed old man says
    you will return the favor someday
    we'll celebrate once this is over

kisses me on the mouth lest there's doubt
    as to what he has in mind
    and how he means to collect the debt

towering over me he hugs me like he owns me
    as if we were in the poster
    for a black-and-white film from his youth

we both pretend that
    the threat frightens me
    not him

THE BODY LAUGHS, PENS A POEM

my body's betrayed me
    in every way imaginable
    it never seems to run out of ideas

it swells puffs up and flakes
    cricks sticks and contorts
    bleeds as it pleases
    it's creative — I must put up

I do not have a body
    I am my body

I read this sentence aloud

my body laughed from the heart
    across the lungs kidneys and ovaries
    all the way to the colon

it sat down
    and penned this poem

The poems "Govorim" (I speak), "Heroina" (Heroine), and "Krotkost" (Tameness) were published in the collection *Promotivni spot za moju domovinu* (2010, A promotional video for my homeland). The poems "Nadmoć" (Domination) and "Tijelo se smije i piše pjesmu" (The body laughs, pens a poem) were published in the collection *Košćela* (2020, Nettle tree). They were translated by Mirza Purić and edited by Si Sophie Pages Whybrew and Dijana Simić.

Senses of Affective Worldmaking

Affective Assemblages: Queer Worldmaking as Critically Reparative Reading

Claudia Breger

In their 1998 article "Sex in Public," Lauren Berlant and Michael Warner describe "queer culture" as "a world-making project," with the emphasis that "'world,' like 'public,' differs from community or group" in that it "includes more people" and spaces "than can be identified," and "modes of feeling that can be learned rather than experienced as a birthright" (558). Thus, they introduce the concept of worldmaking to outline a process of countercultural agency in an asymmetrical public sphere, in which the "taken-for-granted" institutions, narratives, and feelings of heteronormative culture "share an appearance of plenitude" generally unavailable to the more "fragile and ephemeral" expressions of queer culture (558–559; 561). With reference to phenomenological social theory, Berlant and Warner map queer worldmaking as a mobile "space of entrances, exits, unsystematized lines" and "projected horizons" that fails to congeal into "community or identity" but aims to provide "[n]on-standard intimacies" with a "less fleeting" existence: "public in the sense of accessible, available to memory, and sustained through collective activity" (559; 562). Similarly, José Esteban Muñoz's *Disidentifications* (1999) uses the notion of worldmaking—here with reference to Nelson Goodman's constructivist classic *Ways of Worldmaking*—to highlight the "ability" of minoritarian performances "to establish" counterpublics as "alternate views of the world" (195). Even in *de*constructing majoritarian culture, these performances "build an alternative reality" and accomplish "nothing short of the actual making of worlds" (196; 200).

From my perspective, it is this intertwining of constructivist *and* ontological, experiential *and* agential emphases that makes the concept so promising for cultural and aesthetic theory. To be sure, worldmaking's increasing rise to prominence in literary, media, and cultural theory over the past couple of decades has been very heterogeneous, with diverging philosophical roots and many politically less-than-exciting applications. However, connecting productive impulses from different traditions has allowed me to develop a syncretic model that, I argue, unfolds worldmaking's queer (and more generally counterhegemonic) potential for the context of aesthetic worldmaking practices in different media environments. My own work on the topic to date has, with some specificity, mostly focused on literature and cinema and aimed to attend to their medial affordances (see Breger 2017; 2018; 2020). However, the model as such can be adapted to other media environments, perhaps with the caveat that it underlines the political potential of complex and detailed engagements and thus more smoothly resonates with the extensive forms, for example, of serial TV or theater performance than with those of individual Twitter posts. But perhaps we could also rethink larger social media streams and networks in resonant ways?

One of the underlying key ideas of my syncretic conceptualization can be highlighted by spelling the concept with a set of brackets: *world(mak)ing*. The backdrop here is that, in film studies and literary narrative theory, notions of world*mak*ing have been most influentially delineated by cognitive theorists. Their uses of the concept tend to privilege presumably "classical" forms of narrative with coherent plots and stable, goal-oriented characters. For cognitivists, affect mostly comes into play in the form of clear-cut, evaluatively grounded emotions and corresponding audience engagements of empathy, sympathy, or antipathy, which are ideally rewarded by straightforward narrative resolutions (e.g., Herman; Petterson; Plantinga). But these are forms that do not leave much room for the dynamic, tenuous, counterhegemonic assertions pursued by Berlant, Warner, and Muñoz. Perhaps unsurprisingly then, many queer theorists remain skeptical of narrative as such, citing its supposed linearity, teleology, and heteronormativity (see Warhol and Lanser 8). My solution to this conundrum is to infuse the concept of worldmaking with the nonlinear "worlding" energies that have been foregrounded in Deleuzian affect studies. Rather than clear-cut emotions, Deleuzian scholars have underlined the ways in which affective "intensity" disrupts narrative and sociolinguistic codings (Massumi, *Parables* 28)." Instead of storyworlds populated and generated by individuals with intentions, they are interested in affective flows as bodily processes of *"becoming"* or (often with reference to Spinozist philosophy) *worlding*, unfolding in unstable fields of "transindividual entanglement" that precede or exceed seemingly autonomous individuals.[1]

I reconceptualize narrative world(mak)ing, then, as a performative process of affective encounter and *multidimensional, 'multivectoral' assemblage*. This emphatically includes the non-linear forms associated with modernism and postmodernism into the domain of narrative, along with genres and modes of spectacular, theatrical, or bodily "excess"—musical, melodrama, camp, splatter...—and contemporary forms such as Berlant's "situation" that respond to the "waning" of more traditional genres (Berlant, *Cruel Optimism* 5–6). Simultaneously, my definition of world(mak)ing underlines how even the composition and reception of comparatively "straightforward" stories proceed through multivectoral processes of affective association: as I write, read, act, direct, or watch, my narratives are co-composed by the affective charges and (personal and public) memory and fantasy snippets that attach to words, images, gestures, or sounds. In short, affective narrative worldmaking assemblages configure the heterogeneous stuff of affects, associations, experiences, evaluations, forms, intertextual links, matter, perspectives, perceptions, sensations, interpretations,

---

1   Seigworth and Gregg 3; their emphasis; Massumi, *The Power* 14, see also 107–108 on worlding. Seigworth and Gregg reference Spinoza in this context for his discussion of the "affectual composition of a world" (always in the singular) in the "force-relations" between bodies (3; their emphasis). Massumi underlines that, for Spinoza, affects are basically "ways of connecting," indicating "embeddedness in a larger field of life" (110).

topoi, and tropes in and through different media. In the realms of aesthetic worldmaking—be it literature, film, or live performance—these processes of narrative assemblage are firmly anchored in the rhetorical loops of composition (or production) and reading (or spectatorship).

The Deleuzian notion of assemblage is helpful to me in that it designates processes of complex, multiple connections between radically heterogeneous but always already entangled elements, including "bodies" and "utterances, modes of expression, and whole regimes of signs" (Deleuze 177). The latter is important in that some of Deleuze's other work and its reception in affect studies have been marked by very oppositional mappings of 'bodies/affect vs. signification,' or ontology and rhetoric (see, e.g., Massumi, *Parables* 27–28; *The Power*, 105). This, however, undertheorizes affect's own socio-symbolic entanglements, for example, the ways in which even inchoate surges of anxiety (or joy) or unintentional bodily gestures of shame can be shaped by heteronormative culture. Thus, with respect to aesthetic texts, speaking of assemblages helps me to theorize the ways in which (such) affects attach to words in literary texts—and vice versa, socio-semiotic meanings to audiovisual spectacle or bodily performance.

In the context of gender and queer studies, my use of the concept also follows Jasbir Puar's critique of the static metaphor of intersectionality and call to supplement it with assemblage's ability to foreground instability, process, and change ("Queer Times;" "I Would"). My model of affective narrative assemblages thus makes conceptual room for the complexity and instability of identification and affective response and the ways in which literary texts, films, or other aesthetic texts reconfigure hegemonic structures of feeling by unfolding incongruous, layered, conflicting, and unexpected feelings. For example, sudden bursts, or slivers, of affect at odds with positionality-based alignments or dominant narrative invitations to empathize can open up different forms of belonging. As indicated, however, productive instability does not equal the complete absence of narrative. If Deleuzian approaches to affect have often emphasized affect's potential of disruption over everything else,[2] I underline the concept of worlding also for its counter-emphasis: as a process of "linking things" by "sensing them out" (Stewart 342). In worlding, affect's "interrupting" force simultaneously induces a "rebeginning of the world" (Massumi, *The Power*, 107–108). I argue that we can productively link worlding's multivectoral interplay of disruption and (temporal) connection to queer studies' discussions about nonlinear, layered temporalities. For example, it resonates with Elizabeth Freeman's discussion of "form" as "that" which "turns us backward to prior moments, forward to embarrassing utopias, sideways" to seemingly "banal" forms of "being" (Freeman xiii). Or, returning to Muñoz's more programmatic conceptualization, the temporal as well as spatial multivectorality of narrative world(mak)ing might facilitate the counterhegemonic "work" of "looking beyond" our "toxic" present and reimaging "collective futurity," not least in drawing on a "queer past" (Muñoz, *Cruising* 27–28).

Another important aspect of my syncretic model of affective world-making assemblages is that it clears a path between intentionalist (cognitive and rhetorical) models, on the one hand, and the "non-subject-oriented politics" (Puar, "I would" 50) of Deleuzian and other posthumanist approaches, on the other hand. Drawing on Bruno Latour's Actor-Network-Theory, along with contemporary feminist and queer phenomenologies, I argue that affective worldmaking is always undertaken *collectively* by *nonsovereign* actors. On one level, the emphasis on collectivity aims to give significance to the empirical plurality of human participants involved not only in the making of a film or performance, but even the composition, distribution, and reception of "single-authored" pieces of literature or art, from agents and editors to various lay and professional audiences. On another level, the involvement of the collective designates how each individual participant's actions are (in Latour's catchy wordings) *"overtaken"* or *"other-taken"* rather than sovereign in the sense of autonomous or free from external control (Latour, *Reassembling* 45; his emphases). While Latour's theory of non-sovereign action can be located in a long lineage

---

2   See e.g. Massumi, *Parables*, 28; 2015; see critically Brinkema vii.

of subject-critical interventions from psychoanalysis and modernist sociology to Deleuzian posthumanism, his emphasis on the networks entangling humans with other humans as well as "nonhuman" actors is helpful for spelling out the complexity of the processes at stake. The networked character of action entails the interfaces between human, keyboard, camera, microphones, and other technology that have been underlined by Latourian media theory, but also, again, the variously non- or partially conscious assemblages of affects, memories, fantasies, and discourse elements circulating through the bodies and brains of authors, directors, and audiences. It further encompasses the constraints and affordances of the market, financing, genre norms, circulation contexts, and audience expectations; and finally, it allows us to give weight to characters and narrative agents as significant nodes of (overtaken) action (see, e.g., Felski).

My model does not take this emphasis on non-sovereignty in a radically posthumanist direction. In the assemblages of divergent desires and normativities, non-sovereign affective worldmaking processes regularly operate below the individual's full consciousness and beyond their control, but this does not mean that we ought to bypass the sensations, experiences, and active responses of these human actors. Feminist and queer phenomenologies have been crucial in orienting us towards the ways in which transindividual affective circulations shape individual and collective perceptions, alignments, and identifications.[3] In attending to these processes, we can acknowledge non-sovereign agency as embodied and affective as well as political and (more or less) ethical (see also Butler 47–48). Latour himself underlines a resonant methodological orientation in the call to "follow the actors" and deploy their "own world-making abilities," for example, by "listening to what people are saying" about "why they are deeply *attached, moved, affected* by the works of arts which 'make them' feel things."[4]

---

3   See Sedgwick; Ahmed, *The Cultural Politics of Emotion*; *Queer Phenomenology*; Berlant, *Cruel Optimism*.

4   Latour, *Reassembling*, 12, 161, 236 (Latour's emphasis). For a resonant reading of Latour see, in particular, Felski.

As indicated by these quotes, the commitment to tracing non-sovereign agency intersects with broader reorientations towards reparative and "postcritical" reading methodologies in the humanities. Encouraging us to shed the "intellectual baggage" of the prevailing "hermeneutics of suspicion" and its "paranoid" reading practices, Eve Sedgwick introduced the notion of reparative reading as a (carefully phenomenological) methodology of "imaginative close reading," unpacking "local, contingent relations" between knowledge fragments and narrative contexts (145, 124).[5] The reparative position, Sedgwick spells out, is grounded in negative feelings or the full acknowledgment of negative world realities, but its orientation is "to assemble or 'repair'" in a spirit of "love," of the *seeking of pleasure*," self-care, empathy and/or ethical recognition of the other as "once good" (128, 137; Sedgwick's emphasis). Drawing on Sedgwick as well as Latour's forceful criticism of scholarly critique, Ann Cvetkovich, Rita Felski, Heather Love, and others have since similarly urged us to reflexively ground our reading practices in a full spectrum of (negative and positive) affects, in close attention to textual detail and complexity, as well as respect for other voices.[6] Others, to be sure, have objected, insisting on the importance of forceful critique precisely in our moment of increasingly less egalitarian neoliberalism and the rise of new fascisms (e.g., Harcourt). As I write at the end of 2020, postcritical insistences on generosity and love may, in fact, strain many of our queer, feminist, anti-racist, political sensitivities more than a few years ago. How on earth should or could we rely on tracing others' worldmaking processes with patience and empathy in the face of intensified asymmetrical precarity and raging culture wars of today's heightened racisms, interarticulated with renewed violent transphobia, sexually repressive agendas, and the right's absurd "anti-genderist" crusades?

---

5   Sedgwick cites Paul Ricoeur's notion of the "hermeneutics of suspicion" and develops the concept of the reparative from Melanie Klein's psychoanalysis.

6   Latour, "Why Has Critique Run out of Steam?", Cvetkovich; Felski, *The Limits*; *Anker and Felski, eds.*; Love.

Then again, careful attention to detail, nuance, layers, and the attempt to make sense of people's anxiety, anger, and hate may simultaneously be more needed than ever. Even as we need radical change or revolution, Cvetkovich emphasizes, an orientation at affective worldmaking processes does not deliver "magic bullet solutions, ... just the slow steady work of resilient survival, utopian dreaming, and other affective tools for transformation" (2). Already in the 2000s, Muñoz underlined that queer worldmaking entails "both a critique and" a "reparative gesture" (*Cruising* 118). In facilitating layered readings of specific worldmaking practices, my own methodology aims to finetune situational imbrications of such critical and reparative modes in sorting through complex, often incongruous, and almost always unstable assemblages, for example, of anger, anxiety, hate, despair, longing, and optimism. In political orientation, this implies, among other things, that I harbor few illusions about the productivity of (naïve) dialogue with the proponents of right-wing ideology while I do put some faith in the slow work of trying to make sense of the worldmaking orientations even of Trump or *Alternative für Deutschland* (Alternative for Germany) voters.

In the realm of literature, this work turns to and lets itself be inspired by novels such as Ocean Vuong's *On Earth We're Briefly Gorgeous* (2019), with its haunting direct address to the narrator's (traumatized, abusive) "monster" mother (13) and its powerful exploration of the protagonist's layered (desiring, painful, angry, tender, violent) relationship with Trevor, a white, "redneck" (155) kid living amidst addiction in a trailer home. A reparative perspective, Cvetkovich underlines, "embraces conflict rather than separating out right from wrong" in such "generational, racial" and "sexual" mesh-ups, displacing the critical rush to "metacommentary" with "new forms of description that are more textured, more localized, and also less predictably foregone in their conclusions" (10–12). In tracing how affect momentarily dissolves but also turns into identity ("two complete bodies without subjects;" "you are the hunted, a hurt he can't refuse," 156, see also 122), Vuong's narrator fears that they are "not telling you a story as much as a shipwreck" (190). But, as I have argued in this piece, the aesthetic and political power of queer worldmaking assemblages may be, precisely in their ability and commitment to make visible and take time for these "pieces" of "floating" experience (190), imaginatively deploying the pressure they exert on hegemonic identities in carefully mapping, vividly imagining, and forcefully giving weight to alternative worlds of queer, anti-racist coalition building and solidarity.

Bibliography

Ahmed, Sara. *The Cultural Politics of Emotion*. Edinburgh UP, 2004.

——. *Queer Phenomenology*. Duke UP, 2006.

Anker, Elizabeth S. and Rita Felski, editors. *Critique and Postcritique*. Duke UP, 2017.

Berlant, Lauren. *Cruel Optimism*. Duke UP, 2011.

——, and Michael Warner. "Sex in Public." *Critical Inquiry*, vol. 24, no. 2, 1998, pp. 547–566.

Breger, Claudia. "Affects in Configuration: A New Approach to Narrative Worldmaking." *Narrative*, vol. 25, no. 2, 2017, pp. 227–251.

——. "Cosmopolitanism, Controversy, and Collectivity: Zadie Smith's Networked Narration." *Edinburgh Companion to Narrative Theories*, edited by Zara Dinnen and Robyn Warhol. Edinburgh UP, 2018, pp. 83–98.

——. *Making Worlds: Affect and Collectivity in Contemporary European Cinema*. Columbia UP, 2020.

Butler, Judith. *Notes Towards a Performative Theory of Assembly*. Harvard UP, 2015.

Cvetkovich, Ann. *Depression: A Public Feeling*. Duke UP, 2012.

Deleuze, Gilles. "Eight Years Later: 1980 Interview." *Two Regimes of Madness: Texts and Interviews 1975-1995*, edited by David Lapoujade. Translated by Ames Hodges and Mike Taormina. Semiotext(e), 2006, pp. 175–180.

Felski, Rita. *The Limits of Critique*. The University of Chicago Press, 2015.

Freeman, Elizabeth. *Time Binds: Queer Temporalities, Queer Histories*. Duke UP, 2010.

Goodman, Nelson. *Ways of Worldmaking*. Hackett, 1978.

Harcourt, Bernard E., and Didier Fassin, editors. *A Time for Critique.* Columbia UP, 2019.

Herman, David. *Basic Elements of Narrative.* Wiley-Blackwell, 2009.

Latour, Bruno. *Pandora's Hope: Essays on the Reality of Science Studies.* Harvard UP, 1999.

——. *Reassembling the Social: An Introduction to Actor-Network-Theory.* Oxford UP, 2005.

——. "Why Has Critique Run Out of Steam?" *Critical Inquiry*, vol. 30 no.2, 2004, pp. 225–248.

Love, Heather. "Close but not Deep: Literary Ethics and the Descriptive Turn." *New Literary History*, vol. 41, no. 2, 2010, pp. 371–391.

Massumi, Brian. *Parables for the Virtual: Movement, Affect, Sensation.* Duke UP, 2002.

——. *The Power at the End of the Economy.* Duke UP, 2015.

Muñoz, José Esteban. *Disidentifications: Queers of Color and the Performance of Politics.* University of Minnesota Press, 1999.

——. *Cruising Utopia: The Then and There of Queer Futurity.* New York UP, 2009.

Pettersson, Bo. *How Literary Worlds Are Shaped: A Comparative Poetics of Literary Imagination.* de Gruyter, 2018.

Plantinga, Carl. *Moving Viewers: American Film and the Spectator's Experience.* The University of California Press, 2009.

Puar, Jasbir. "'I would rather be a cyborg than a goddess': Becoming-Intersectional in Assemblage Theory." *PhiloSOPHIA: A Journal of Feminist Philosophy*, vol. 2, no. 1 2012, pp. 49–66.

——. "Queer Times, Queer Assemblages." *Social Text*, vol. 23, no. 3–4, 2005, pp. 121–139.

Sedgwick, Eve Kosofsky. *Touching Feeling: Affect, Pedagogy, Performativity.* Duke UP, 2003.

Seigworth, Gregory J. and Melissa Gregg. "An Inventory of Shimmers." *The Affect Theory Reader*, edited by Melissa Gregg and Gregory J. Seigworth. Duke UP, 2010, pp. 1–25.

Stewart, Kathleen. "Afterword: Worlding Refrains." *The Affect Theory Reader*, edited by Melissa Gregg and Gregory Seigworth pp. 339–353.

Vuong, Ocean. *On Earth We're Briefly Gorgeous: A Novel*. Penguin Press, 2019.

Warhol, Robyn and Susan S. Lanser. Introduction. *Narrative Theory Unbound: Queer and Feminist Interventions*, edited by Robyn Warhol and Susan S. Lanser. The Ohio State UP, 2015, pp. 1–20.

What World is Made?:
Gender and Affect in Three Life Moments

May Friedman

How can I write about the affective experiences of being a woman without resorting to essentialism or trite platitudes? If, as Eugenie Shinkle surmises, affect is "characterised in part by its resistance to sociolinguistic qualification; as a category, it resists critique and lacks a precise theoretical vocabulary" (75), can I use the imprecision of language to try to evoke the body, the "heartmind" (Loveless) of my experiences of femininity and that world that my gendered experiences create? If worldmaking is grounded in "affect, emotion, and perception" (Breger 232), how can I engage in the nuances of the construction of my own gendered world?

While my sense of myself as a racialized cisgender woman has shifted and morphed, there is no doubt that the strictures of womanhood have girded my life. They have implicated my body, my aesthetics; they have governed my relationships and engagements with others; they have journeyed alongside my professional roles and behaviors. In many respects, I have followed the "happiness scripts" that Sara Ahmed delineates (*Promise of Happiness*), and yet shame lurks in the fissures and tensions between my experiences of normative femininity and my authentic understandings of myself.

Ultimately, my experiences of womanhood are variegated and intersected, reminding me that there is no essential characteristic to womanhood—not biology, not family composition, not aptitude or character trait—but that, at the same time, every part of my life is imprinted by and through my experiences of gender. My world is a woman's world, and also—each woman's world is distinct. How can I strain against the stickiness of affect to consider my experiences of femininity and womanhood in the specifics of key life moments?

Love

Is there a more gendered space than a heterosexual wedding? At the time of my own long-ago nuptials, queer marriages were still illegal in my jurisdiction, and so my massive, poofy wedding was about as straight a space as could be imagined. My ambivalence about gender roles was conveniently concealed under my enormous dress, along with my fat belly. My imminent in-laws, confused by our henna party days before, were soothed by this more familiar specter of white dress and black tie. Hundreds of friends and family members joined us to celebrate. Yes, we were celebrating love—love that has, against all odds, flourished for more than two decades—but also the spectacle of gendered behaviors.

What world was established through this performance, an imperfect performance at best? On the one hand, I was the exemplar of a particular version of womanhood: marrying young; in a ceremony and spectacle traditional to my culture, my community. I remember feeling relieved that I had avoided some kind of smothering shame by outrunning spinsterhood, a feeling that I recognize as bizarre coming from an educated woman in her early twenties at the turn of the twenty-first century. And yet—throughout my young life, normative femininity [read: marriage] was presented as a requirement (for that matter, so was shame). To consider a life that transgressed this framework was literally unthinkable; in some ways, it remains so.

These moments return to me in affective registers. My dress, his suit. The discomfort of my too-tight undergarments, raising welts on my flesh in an effort to constrain my bulges. The private knowledge of my ambiguous relationship with queer identity. The sweat and flush on my face as I was required, as an introvert, to interact, fully, enthusiastically, for hours. The dancing whirl of my macho uncle forcibly goose-stepping me around the dance floor, his arm like a binding seat belt across my back. I am reminded of Isobel Armstrong's words that

> Affect . . . in an ambiguous, alternating force . . . belongs to a chain of discourse and breaks it: it alternates between being bound and un-bound, attached to signification and rupturing it. It is essentially an energy of the "between" . . . Thus it has the role of conjoining and dis-joining, making and unmaking . . . The concealing and revealing, ex-posing and masking process which belongs to affect is structurally tied to the possibility of meaning. (123)

This wedding was about signification, but also about rupture. I was rendered intelligible to those around me (in my approach to both womanhood and whiteness, albeit always imperfectly), but ultimately *un*intelligible to myself.

I wonder what I would say to that young woman—so long ago. Would I tell her to recognize this moment as the spectacle it was, to relish its irony and performance without getting too caught up in con-cerns about authenticity? Would I tell her to remember what really mat-tered in that moment—the birthplace of a family—rather than all the trappings and strangulations that the day held? Would I offer a more comfortable bra, at least—release for the body if not the mind? That unformed person, scarcely aware of the many discourses layered on the raced and gendered body whirling around that dance floor, might not have wanted to consider those constraints, but I believe that even then, my young self knew that for all the joy of the moment, something was askew.

Loss

My affective experience of gender does not center on what my body has or has not done, nor the parts it does or does not possess. At the same time, my experiences of womanhood have been marked by the particular taboos aimed at body functions, including the specificities of pregnancy loss. In particular, as a cis woman, my experiences of pregnancy and reproduction have been imprinted with gendered expectations. While in no way suggesting that the womb is the seat of womanhood then, I wonder how to narrate my own embodied experiences in the moment where my womb failed?

While I have borne living children, I have also experienced periods of grave loss. After a much-desired pregnancy was interrupted when no heartbeat could be detected halfway through gestation, I found myself in the awful position of having to figure out how to birth an unfinished being. Having birthed my living children at home, I was hospitalized, medicalized, subject to endless manipulation and scrutiny.

I was struck by both the mundanity and grotesquerie of loss. On the one hand, this was in no way a unique tragedy—as I already knew, pregnancies end constantly. Loss is a part of all life and certainly part of reproductive life. Despite the mundanity of the experiences, it was nonetheless spectacular—in the sense of inviting spectacle—in the affective realm. The chafe of the hospital gown that I bitterly resisted but was finally forced to don—the clang of the alarm I pulled when, unexpectedly, I gave birth while I was alone in the bathroom—the scarlet blood, the rough skin of my cheeks salted by tears. This was both more and less than a medical situation—a regrettable but uncomplicated series of procedures, but also the death of hope, of a particular version of myself as mother to this specific child, of the sibling my children had anticipated. At the heart of it was the womb, behaving in troublesome ways—clenching out tissue at the "wrong" time, then holding on to residue that necessitated surgical removal. My sense of myself as mother, as woman, as patient, as mourner, was all held in the womb at that time.

Like so much of my experience of womanhood, this moment lives between the body and the mind, in the interplay between physical sensation and emotional reaction. I found myself feeling all the shame of a failed body, the trauma of a loss, in ways that were inarticulate but deeply held. I felt an overwhelming sense of abjection: the "rejection of bodies, or aspects of bodies, that threaten cultural norms about how human bodies should look and behave" (Rice 197), even as I acknowledged that this was terribly, painfully normal.

How do we acknowledge the complicated and messy terrain of the uterine environment without resorting to essentialism—to hysteria? How can I acknowledge that my womb is an organ like no other, even now as it enters retirement? How can I understand myself as a woman independent of biology and also acknowledge my uterus as it does its work, succeeds, and fails at giving life? The complexities of womb and woman elude words and one another. All I know is the steady drip of blood.

Labor

I am a reluctant and uneasy scholar. Throughout my childhood and young adulthood, my only consistent ambition was motherhood; all other possibilities seemed ancillary. Perhaps the same gendered training that dampened my ambition is also partially to blame for my rampant imposter syndrome, the overwhelming and abiding feeling that I am getting away with something by taking a seat at the table. Somewhere in the blend of children and academia, there is a specific embodied discomfort—the frequent exhortations of "I don't know how you do it!" suggesting, somehow, that I can't be doing it very well.

In this space, which is meant to be sterile and driven by the mind, I nonetheless feel my gendered body deeply. I remember Ahmed's reflections on the embodiment of feelings, "Emotion is the feeling of bodily change. The immediacy of the "is" suggests that emotions do not involve processes of thought, attribution or evaluation: we feel fear, for example, because our heart is racing, our skin is sweating. Emotions involve appraisals, judgements, attitudes" (*Cultural Politics of Emotion* 5). I remember the flush on my cheeks as a colleague asks, not for the first time, "HOW many children do you have now?"; the shame in my belly when I reveal, yet again, that I am not the departmental assistant; the rise of pride and anger at the backhanded praise when I say something sensible at a meeting. I think often of a shirt I once saw that read, "Lord, give me the confidence of a mediocre white man." In the absence of that confidence, I ache, I long, I fear. Shinkle writes that

[a]ffect is transformative precisely because of its ability to move between the intimate, the idiosyncratic and the individual, and the public or institutional. It is in the *mattering* of perception that images become political: paying attention to the affective and embodied dimensions of image perception can lead to new ways of understanding how
such images can embody not conformity, but political divergence. (85,
emphasis in original)

In other words—my shame and anger *matter*; may have transformative
potential. A consideration of my emotional and embodied responses
elicits more information about racism and sexism, about institutional-
ized normative frames. In this emotional register, I may find pathways
for survival on both personal and institutional levels, remembering that
"it is about finding ways to exist in a world that makes it difficult to exist" (Ahmed, *Living a Feminist Life* 239).

On a more mundane level, I see the ways I am enacting stereotypically feminine and maternal behaviors in my academic roles. I am responsible for a high degree of emotional labor on behalf of my students
and, sometimes, my colleagues. I am in service roles that are heavy on
workload and light on prestige. Some of the most painful moments of
awareness come in the ways that my identities as woman, mother, academic rub together, sometimes coherently, sometimes in tension: the
ways that my students very sweetly feel entitled to my time and care, for
issues both academic and personal. The extent to which consciousness-
raising work is built into my life—as a fat brown mother, I see-saw between feeling like helping people grapple with issues of privilege and
oppression is the most important activist work I do and feeling sick of
being everyone's Mammy. COVID has made these tensions more palpa-
ble, especially in the intersectional realm of gender. I gaze at my brown
skin on the zoom screen and remember, again, why I don't think I "look
like" an academic. Despite tenure, I feel the desperation of blending
parenting and work at this moment, of turning off my video to attend
to a child's leaky nose, feeling the endless and impossible ache of being
a woman, a mother, and a worker at the present moment.

What is the politics of recognition when brown, first generation students need me, see themselves in me, but my established white colleagues do not? What counterpublic is created in the tensions between recognition, power, and the body?

What World is Made?

If emotional work is ultimately ineffable, then perhaps my experience of navigating womanhood can only be conveyed in the affective register. The world that is created is, in Claudia Breger's words, filled with "plural, sensory and conceptual truths" (235). Perhaps my commitment to convoluted life writing, arts-based approaches, and storied care is bound up in my need to bathe in complexity—rather than reducing gender, relationships, loss, livelihood into the realm of essentialism and truism. In thinking through my experiences of womanhood and affect, I reject the supposition that femininity is the seat of emotion—that women have big feelings. Rather, the "work of affect" (Breger 234) offers a lens into the productive potential of worldmaking, the creation of a world unspooling, in process, rather than the construction of a static and unyielding thing. Instead, I note that my own relationship with womanhood is an assemblage, like my body, that is scarred, stretched, and ultimately imperfect, rife with contradiction and rupture.

Bibliography

Ahmed, Sara. *The Promise of Happiness*. Duke UP, 2010.
——. *The Cultural Politics of Emotion*, 2nd ed., Edinburgh UP, 2014.
——. *Living a Feminist Life*. Duke UP, 2017.
Armstrong, Isobel. *The Radical Aesthetic*. Wiley Blackwell, 2000.
Breger, Claudia. "Affects in Configuration: A New Approach to Narrative Worldmaking." *Narrative*, vol. 25, no. 2, 2017, pp. 227–251.
Loveless, Natalie. *How to Make Art at the End of the World*. Duke UP, 2019.

Rice, Carla. *Becoming Women: The Embodied Self in Image Culture*. University of Toronto Press, 2014.

Shinkle, Eugenie. "Uneasy Bodies: Affect, Embodied Perception and Contemporary Fashion Photography." *Carnal Aesthetics: Transgressive Imagery and Feminist Politics*, edited by Bettina Papenburg and Marta Zarzycka, I.B. Tauris & Co. Ltd., 2012, pp. 73–88.

Why Our Knees Kiss

Deborah D.E.E.P. Mouton

They say it's rickets, bone malformation, some genetic accident. They don't know the real reason some of our knees kiss, and our thighs rub close. It isn't a defect. Those rumors came out of envy.

Way back, when the ground was fertile, and the sugar cane was sweet, the Speight women, those on my mother's side, thrived. They descended from the Baartmans and were the wisest and most beautiful in all of the South. They were the first adapters. The way a child masters a familiar song by ear is the same way the Speights took to languages. They held a library on their tongues. The most notorious thinker of them all was Lula.

Lula was a griot. That meant she carried the history of thousands of years in the grooves of her teeth. While out harvesting crops, she would whisper stories to the other workers of how the sun and moon loved so hard that they began to share each other's light. Back on the plantation, the children would gather to listen to the symphony of stories strum from her mouth. Though it wasn't always safe. The same way the Speights came together to devour their food, other hungry beasts waited for an opening to devour too.

Alligators lived on the edge of the plantation. They gained an appetite for bait babies and couldn't shake the craving. They would hide in the high grass and wait for the children to wander too far from their parents. Then, they would wrestle them under and swallow them whole. But the Speight women were smarter than the gators. They grew their hips and butts round as the perfect way to keep the children high. They would allow the children to scale their bottoms and hold onto their backs. This way, when the meadow grass got unyielding, they could see the gators coming and avoid being eaten.

This angered the gators. They much preferred the taste of melanin over turtles or deer. They plotted and schemed for a way to lure the children back to the swampy ground. Lula worried for the children's safety; she had grown fond of every fire-lit cherub face who filled themselves with story. She knew one day they would pass them on, make stories of their own. So, one day, while Lula was hunting, she overheard the gators coming up with a plan. They were going to strike in the evening; when Lula sat all the children down to listen to the last story of the night, they would creep into the village. They would strike at Lula's most interesting part. While all the children were leaning in, completely entranced by Lula, they would let their guards down. Then, the gators would feast. The gators thought this was a solid plan, though they didn't count on Lula's wit.

Lula gathered the women and told them what she had heard out in the highest grass. They knew the gators had to be stopped and began brainstorming a plan of their own. One woman suggested singing all the gators to sleep in Nama since the clicks served as their own luring drumbeat. Another said to build a wall too high for the gators to climb but then remembered the dangers of walls. Lula combed the archives of her mouth and said she had a crazy idea. Back when the waters stood still, the Speight women watched the stagnant ocean begin to stink. They spoke to the moon and told her that the land would perish if the water didn't begin to move. So, in an effort to help, the Speight woman lent their bodies to the sea's aid. They stood on the coastline and rocked their hips like an ebb and flow. The water hesitated. Then they realized if they pressed their knees together, the friction of their hips set off its own trance. Before they knew it, the waves were rising and falling to the motion of their hips. This hypnotism was the perfect way to stop the gators.

The women all agreed that if their hips could protect their children and teach the waves how to come and go, they must be powerful enough to confuse the gators. Lula brought each woman a piece of twine to tie around her knees. Then they lined the perimeter as the sun began to set.

Lula gathered the children like always and began to tell them a story. The gators approached. They made it past the first line of shanties, but as they broke into the center, the rhythmic sway took over. The women completely shielded the children. Their magnetic orbit, lulling and powerful. The gators, on sight, began to rock without even realizing it. Before long, they were dizzy and confused and forgot why they were there in the first place. The nausea set in next, sending every gator scurrying back beneath the crest out of queasiness and confusion.

The women rejoiced. And every time the persistent gators would try to get too close, the women would tie their knees and move like the waves. Before long, they no longer needed the rope. As most things adapt, so did the women. Their round hips and large bottoms swayed over kissing knees to keep all of them safe and sound. But there was always another threat lurking. Some came through the Colonies' hills. Some sailed through the sea, convinced to capture the power of the trance.

But you, my dear, still hold it. In the space where your knees kiss and your thighs spark fire. The way to tame this world. And nothing about your body, about your joy, is an accident.

Affective Worldmaking in Times of Crisis: An Interview

Silvia Schultermandl and Ann Cvetkovich

In a presentation on Jan 14, 2021, as part of the international symposium "Affective Worldmaking: Narrative Counterpublics of Gender and Sexuality," Ann Cvetkovich gave a public lecture on "Public Feelings in a Time of Pandemic." Her talk drew on writing that she has been doing over the course of the pandemic in monthly meetings with the Austin (Texas)-based Public Feelings group. These short pieces constitute efforts to make sense of what is going on—or just document how it feels—with attention to topics such as COVID silver linings (and other pandemic keywords); Zoom-based art and performance; protest under conditions of social distancing; dialectics of hope and despair; black feminist resources for survival and other forms of collective care and mutual aid; and the relation between the HIV/AIDS pandemic and the COVID-19 pandemic. Through an exploration of the current state of theories of affect and sensation, she explored the differences and connections between how the pandemic feels in Canada/US and how it feels in Austria/Europe.

In the following interview, Silvia Schultermandl invites Ann Cvetkovich to discuss theoretical and methodological connections between her recent work on public feelings and the symposium's focus on affective worldmaking.

Silvia: The edited volume in which this interview appears theorizes narratives of gender and sexuality. We use affective worldmaking as a methodology through which to explore the potential of various kinds of narrative (present in different media like literature, film, performance, social media) to generate feelings of identity and belonging. Based on your own work, how, would you say, might a focus on gender and sexuality allow for a particular kind of worldmaking?

Ann: I have been so embedded in intersectional forms of thinking that it becomes difficult to think gender and sexuality independently from questions of race and histories of migration, diaspora, capitalism, and colonialism. But an attunement to categories of gender and sexuality prompted my interest in affective worldmaking in the first place, through attention to relationality, intimacy, and the local. Considerations of gender and sexuality, and feminism and queer theory in general, are not the only reasons one would come to that category, but they definitely encourage us to think about worlds—including the question of what constitutes a "world" in worldmaking—through local and ordinary spaces such as those fostered by relations of caretaking and attachment. My focus on how a world can be constructed in very intimate and local ways, when a group of people attempts to make something together, has benefitted tremendously from feminist and queer studies. Critical understandings of the family as a unit of bonding and a place where nation and history converge, to create sites of positive (joy) and negative affects (violence and terror), have been good questions with which to work.

Moreover, questions about affective worldmaking revolve in large part around a structuring question to which affect theory returns: How am I feeling and what can we do with that unit of "data" (which also changes that which counts as "data")? It is useful to answer these questions through recourse to gendered categories of analysis and feminist work on the relationship between the personal and the political. For me, saying something meaningful, with regard to an analysis of geopolitical conditions, by looking at affective experience is a key conceptual move that I think is also at the heart of affective worldmaking.

Silvia: On occasion, you have spoken of your own rituals (mentioning writing, drawing, crafting), especially those within the Feel Tank or your collaborative work with artists. In your book *Depression: A Public Feeling* (2012), you describe these practices as *utopia of ordinary habit*, practices that allow us to cope with negative affects (such as depression, or the pandemic feelings we mentioned in our symposium: anger, fear, anxiety). Do you think of these practices as strategies of affective worldmaking?

Ann: This summarizes nicely the work I have done around what you are calling affective worldmaking, and I am pleased to see you connect it to my notion of the utopia of ordinary habit. I have an abiding interest in forms of collectivity and forms of community. Over the course of my career, there have been many different keywords to describe these phenomena: subcultures; publics and counterpublics; more recently, a turn to the notion of the commons; and worldmaking, whose lineage I track in the work of my fellow travelers Katie Stewart, Lauren Berlant, and José Muñoz. In affect studies, we are seeking vocabulary to describe the affective relationships which emerge from gatherings of people. For me, an important question in relation to the modes of alternative worldbuilding is the nature of the social. I am indebted to the work of my fellow queer theorists who focus on the anti-social or what Lauren Berlant has been calling the "inconvenience of others"—these reminders of how difficult it can be when we get together as a group. For instance, queer theory has applied a critical lens to the category of the family, in particular, its heteronormative iterations but also its homonormative formations.

Silvia: For our project, affective worldmaking not only has a narrative/discursive dimension but also includes a shared practice, a collective action, characterized by everyday rituals. How important are questions of narrative for your work?

Ann: Categories of narrative or the literary and textual have often not been general enough for me, and I find myself cutting across a range of media in order to think about the cultural formations that bring people together. What are the ordinary activities, whether it is feminist forms of crafting, making music together, or dancing together? What different modes of being in a space together are ways of making a community? The linkage between affect and sensation and renewed interest in the sensory dimensions of affective experience also demand that we do not think too narrowly about the category of narrative. In turn, questions about the literary public spheres through which a book might bring us together into a room are important. This is also true for digital spaces where people are trading texts via social media and thereby creating community. In this way, questions about affective worldmaking are also related to questions about narrative and storytelling.

Silvia: In your answers, you have been paying homage to some of your fellow travelers. I wonder if you could briefly explain the significance of the Chicago Feel Tank and the Public Feelings Project in Austin.

Ann: Feel Tank is the group based in Chicago that has included Lauren Berlant, Debbie Gould, Rebecca Zorach, Mary Patten, and Gregg Bordowitz, among others. They came up with the concept of political depression, which in turn catalyzed my work under that rubric. Public Feelings is the name for a group predominantly based in Austin, Texas, whose throughline has been my collaboration with my longtime friend and colleague Katie Stewart. There are a lot of cross-fertilizations between the two groups, such as Katie and Lauren's co-authored book *The Hundreds* (2019).

The Public Feelings project grew out of an effort to think through the 20th anniversary of the infamous 1982 Barnard Conference on Sexuality, an event that was very generative for many of us interested in conflicts within feminism around sexuality. At the turn of the millennium, we wanted to think about a possible future for that work and came up with a number of working groups, one of which was organized around the concept of Public Feelings. Although the first meeting took place before the events of September 11, 2001, the subsequent work under that rubric was catalyzed by an effort to think about the political scene in its aftermath and at the dawning of the 21st century. From there, it has had a life of its own.

All in all, Public Feelings represents a commitment to worldmaking in the form of small cells—I like to use that term from radical politics. Small groups of people who, by virtue of coming together, can think together, be together, and feel together, in order to generate new ideas, and by virtue of that, craft affective worlds and visions of the future. In Austin, Public Feelings began as a reading group, which is a time-honored tradition for generating new and subaltern forms of thinking in academia and in art communities. But eventually, we morphed into a writing group and concocted the format of the writing salon, where we would bring 500 words of writing and share it with each other. It was a very simple format that proved very inspiring and generative; it is an example of the utopia of everyday habit, a very simple practice that can provide people with a reason to come together and generate a kind of vitality or ongoing life. This habit has managed to thrive during conditions of the pandemic, and a small group of us, mostly based in Austin, has managed to meet once a month via Zoom across this past year. That work has fed into talks and events, such as the one I did with your group.

Silvia: During our symposium, you noted a curious 20-year interval of crises: the Reagan years and the advent of neoliberalism; then, 20 years later, 9/11 and the subsequent nationalism, militarism, and surveillance culture; and another 20 years later, the COVID pandemic. I wonder if the caretaking during these distinct crises is different. What do you make of these intervals?

Ann: The 20-year interval was a wonderful insight that emerged from our conversation during the symposium. I am struck by a couple of things: 20 years could be taken as a generational marker, and this connects to questions of care and how we transmit knowledge across generations. Caretaking can include providing resources in the form of experiences and histories —or narratives—from previous generations of struggle.

This notion of 20-year intervals might also index a longer arc of post-WWII capitalism and social movements. For instance, I consider myself to be shaped by the dreams of liberation that emerged with the social and cultural movements of the 1960s and 1970s, which were enabled by a renewed economic vitality that often came at the expense of those in the global South. I think it is important to have histories of alternative cultures, which can take the form of affectively charged oral histories transmitted from one generation to the next. What do we as feminists of a particular generation have to say to those of the next generation? Of late, Black feminisms that have existed inside and outside of academia have found their way into the Black Lives Matter movement and shaped the work of contemporary scholars such as Saidiya Hartman and Christina Sharpe, whose concepts of the "afterlife" or "wake" of slavery have in turn been widely circulated for understanding loss, grief, and mourning. I am thinking here, too, of the transmission across generations of the work of James Baldwin, Audre Lorde, Angela Davis, Octavia Butler, among many others, as resources for survival.

Silvia: In a previous project with the Berlin-based artist Karin Michalski, you created *The Alphabet of Feeling Bad*. How does this notion of taking inventory of public feelings work in terms of its own embedded potential for affective worldmaking? Does it have to do with the creation of lists and structure, or do you consider it more of a praxis of regaining agency through creativity in the face of depression?

Ann: This might be where we come back around to the category of narrative, or at least the word. *The Alphabet of Feeling Bad* project is a form of abecedary which tries to give us expanded vocabularies of affect. The project wants to make room for negative feelings: you get to feel bad, and you still get to be in community with others. This counters the exclusion people often experience when they feel that they don't belong because of their anti-social or non-normative feelings. We also wanted to resist clinical definitions of feeling bad; I am ambivalent about the ubiquity of diagnostic categories like anxiety and depression because I believe that we need a richer vocabulary for how we feel or why we feel bad.

One of the structuring elements for the project is to give people tools for the question "How do you feel"? People sharing how they feel and then building something collective from there can be a form of affective worldmaking. Returning to the power of words, a very generative moment in workshops can take the form of inviting people to make sense of feelings such as being tired or apprehensive. The process of naming is connected to forms of storytelling through which we allow for a more inclusive worldmaking, where feeling bad also comes with the capacity to claim a sense of belonging. Sometimes I begin my classes by inviting everyone to contribute one word to describe how they feel that day, and we create a list of words that describe how the group feels. Each of these words could be a prompt for people to begin telling their stories—a modest practice of collective sharing but nevertheless an important tool for affective worldmaking. The aim is to make asking, and answering, the question "How do you feel?" a meaningful intervention in terms of building both relationships and worlds.

Silvia: Perhaps as a follow-up: can we think of this as emerging counter-archives that record and index instances of feeling bad that otherwise do not find a place in more mainstream worldmaking practices, especially in narratives about the COVID pandemic, the AIDS crisis, or depression in relation to a variety of political events? What would you say is the connection between counter-archive and counterpublics and their transformative potential?

Ann: Bringing in ideas about the archive in the documentation of people's feelings raises a set of methodological questions. This practice often runs counter to more normative or conventional ways of asking people how they feel, particularly survey forms of data. It is interesting to think about ways to make these narratives add up to a form of collective knowledge. I have been fascinated by the form of the pandemic diary—which will no doubt contribute to a compelling archive of this time. I have been involved in the NYC COVID-19 Oral History, Narrative and Memory Archive project at Columbia University in New York, which is collecting contributions from approximately 2000 participants, including interviews and open-ended written questionnaires. The project calls attention to a conundrum: how to create the data sets in a way that also disrupts the process of data collection in order to insist that the documentation of affect is a valuable counter-archive.

Silvia: A concept you have mentioned in several of your recent talks is "COVID silver linings." Connecting to what you said about the emergence of new forms of documenting the present moment and what it feels like, I wonder what a potential counter-archive might look like when we zoom in on this idea of COVID silver linings. As difficult as it might be to acknowledge that there are COVID silver linings, doesn't this also invite us to think about people's positionalities and unevenly distributed access to power and privilege?

Ann: This concept of COVID silver linings has been an ongoing project for me. I first wrote about it in April 2020 during the early weeks of the pandemic, and it read differently in January during your symposium, and it seems different again in April 2021 when we are doing this interview. These shifts are no doubt part of the fluidity and unpredictability of affect in this time of pandemic. The term has been a useful way to hold open questions about the dialectics of hope and despair and of positive and negative affects that have always been at the heart of the public feelings project, as I have understood it. At the same time, I am somewhat ambivalent about the vernacular use of the term COVID silver linings, in so far as it suggests the impulse to move too quickly towards something positive, to putting a happy face on something that is so terrible. Nevertheless, it also registers an inability to know what the pandemic might mean with respect to individual experience, which is, of course, relational and exists across a range of scales and locations.

At this point, one of the open questions for me is: Will one of the COVID silver linings have been the opportunity for a new level of activism around anti-Black racism and understandings of white supremacy, a term which is now circulating in ways that it was not a year ago? For example, is it a COVID silver lining that the term "systemic racism" is rolling off the tongues of ordinary citizens, police officers, and politicians in unprecedented ways? These developments connect to Arundhati Roy's notion of the pandemic as a portal and the questions it raises about whether the pandemic might ultimately take us somewhere else—to a different future. I see this evidenced in the fact that a lot of people are talking about not wanting to go "back to normal"—a version of COVID silver linings that we might want to work with, albeit critically. I used the term COVID silver linings to describe working from home for privileged, middle-class people who have that option. As an extension of that experience, people are now thinking about ways in which the workplace as we know it will be fundamentally transformed. For those of us who work in the university, this is a very open-ended question as we go forward, including speculation about the possible advantages and drawbacks of teaching online or remotely and the kinds of worldmaking we might engage in by doing so.

Silvia: A particular form of affective worldmaking during the pandemic is connected to care. Do times of crisis always demand specific practices of self-care?

Ann: Care has emerged as a central category during the pandemic, and it has been important to tease apart distinctions between collective care and self-care. Even before the pandemic, I was interested in how activists, especially those working to dismantle racism, were drawing new concepts and strategies of self-care from Audre Lorde's statement that "caring for myself is not self-indulgence, it is self-preservation, and that is an act of political warfare." Although there have been critiques of "self-care" and concern that the spirit of Lorde's thinking be honored through understandings of self-care as collectively oriented, I think it's a welcome development to think about care as affective worldmaking and about how we can build collectivities through mutual care.

Affective Be/Longing: Redefining Public Spheres

Textual Encounters of Hope and Be/Longing: Science Fiction and Trans Worldmaking

Si Sophie Pages Whybrew

Introduction: (Re-)Claiming Trans Futures in Science Fiction

Despite its tendency towards conservatism, science fiction has long exhibited an often troubling and hesitant fascination for the possibility of gender transgression. Nevertheless, in the face of mounting evidence about the transcultural and historical existence and increasing visibility of trans people, most science fiction narratives have remained largely allegorical and speculative with regards to the possibility of trans identification, until recently. For example, despite its reputation for inclusion and diversity, it took the Star Trek franchise until 2020 to finally include the show's first two trans and nonbinary characters (played by nonbinary actors) on *Star Trek: Discovery's* third season. However, even then, it placed these characters into a universe that seemingly remains thoroughly cisnormative otherwise.[1]

Nonetheless, trans readers and audiences have exhibited a remarkable ability to read ourselves into narratives that were not meant to include us and reclaim them as a means to sustain our "transgender becoming[s]" (Keegan, "Revisitation" 30).[2] As YouTuber Jessi Earl ob-

---

1   For a more thorough discussion of this phenomenon, see Whybrew, "Transgender and Nonbinary Trek Characters" in The *Routledge Handbook to Star Trek* (Forthcoming 2022).

2   Lucas Cassidy Crawford conceptualized this potential under the heading of "aesthetic transgendering" in his descriptions of trans folks' reclamation of built

serves about the 1992 Star Trek episode "The Outcast": "When I watched this episode as a kid, it helped give me the representation, words, and thoughts to help me begin to understand who I was as a trans person. It helped me feel a little bit less like an outcast" ("Star"). Although this phenomenon, arguably, speaks more to the resilient potential of trans viewers and our ability to read ourselves into these narratives than to the franchise's and the genre's progressive character, it nonetheless highlights science fiction's significance for many trans people and the potential that finding ourselves represented within it may hold for us in a world that all too often remains hostile to our existence. Indeed, while being literally out of this world, for me, the trans adjacent alien allegories of Star Trek represented one of the few glimpses of the possibility of a livable trans existence that did not come laden with the affective weight of feelings of shame and pain within the narrative cosmology of my own childhood. Similarly, despite being regrettably behind the times and including several severe missteps,[3] *Star Trek: Discovery's* tentative first steps toward trans inclusion left me with a hopeful feeling of potentiality and a desire for more.

---

environments that were not meant to include them ("Poetics" 483). Cael M. Keegan has proposed that this might also occur in trans people's interactions with visual media and that it ultimately "reveals how trans phenomenology lies, embedded and unacknowledged, in the architecture of culture itself" ("Revisitation" 30). Through their work, Crawford and Keegan highlight how trans people can uncover trans "forms of meaning that allow transgender phenomena to extend into the world" and how this ultimately may contribute to "extend[ing]" and "sustain[ing]" trajectories of "transgender becoming" (Keegan, "Revisitation" 30).

3   For example, the show's writers killed off the trans masculine character, Gray, mere moments after introducing him, only to have him return as a disembodied spirit that is only visible to his nonbinary partner, Adira, for much of the season (Whybrew, Forthcoming 2022).

Moving towards Trans Science Fiction

Since the 1980s, the increasing social awareness towards trans identities brought about by the work of trans advocacy groups in the United
States and Canada, as well as the theoretical work of queer theory and
trans studies, has resulted in a diversification of North American science fiction stories that include gender-nonconforming or transition-
ing human characters (Melzer 397; Lothian 70). Significantly, this development also resulted in the publication of seven anthologies of trans-
authored and themed science fiction stories since 2012,[4] which I have
had the pleasure of reading and studying for my doctorate. Although
these publications have been limited to small publishers or came about
as a result of crowdfunding projects (Morgan, "Tipping" 95, 99), I argue in my dissertation that their contributors have used the genre's
conventions to explore an unprecedented plurality of affective trans experiences, connections, and associations. Moreover, they envision both
trans worlds of mutual recognition, care, and affirmation and offer the
hopeful promise of and longing for futures in which wider social acceptance is more than just a painfully deferred dream. As a result, these
stories not only represent a significant challenge to the genre's legacy
of trans erasure, but they may also offer more fertile ground for trans
worldmaking than the cis-authored stories that preceded them.

Indeed, in some ways, these narratives may be viewed as literary
extensions of trans rights movements and as examples of a literary
coming-to-voice of the trans communities in North America, as they
are indicative of a new, self-determined register and "oppositional discourse" (hooks, *talking* 29) of trans representation within the science fic-

---

4   Namely, *Beyond Binary: Genderqueer and Sexually Fluid Speculative Fiction* (2012)
     by brit mandelo, the "Queers Destroy Science Fiction!" issue of *Lightspeed* edited
     by Seanan McGuire (2015), K.M. Szpara's *Transcendent: The Year's Best Transgen-
     der Speculative Fiction* (2016), and Bogi Takacs' *Transcendent 2* (2017), *Meanwhile,
     Elsewhere: Science Fiction and Fantasy from Transgender Writers* edited by Cat Fitz-
     patrick and Casey Plett (2017), and *Transcendent 3* (2018) and 4 (2019) also edited
     by Bogi Takacs.

tion genre that may light the way to better pasts, presents, and futures, by illuminating and challenging the violence of the cisnormative status quo. As such, these narratives hold the potential to act as affective and collective resources of hope and be/longing for trans readers, as they offer opportunities for having our identities and experiences affirmed, mirrored, validated, and possibly even celebrated. Such opportunities are often withheld in cisnormative social worlds. In the words of José Esteban Muñoz, they may function as "the warm illumination of a horizon imbued with potentiality" (*Cruising* 1) and, as Belinda Deneen Wallace puts it, "become[] a safe space of belonging where the future is now" (60), or rather, where traces of more bearable worlds might be found.

For, as Muñoz makes clear, worldmaking[5] can create and share "alternate views of the world" that may function as "oppositional ideologies" and "critiques of oppressive regimes of 'truth' that subjugate minoritarian people" (*Disidentification* 195). As a result, trans-authored science fiction stories may function as counterpublics and form a basis for "support," thus contributing to trans community building (Nicolazzo et al. 307). Indeed, these stories may be said to constitute a form of trans worldmaking and function as affective and collective counterpublics for trans readers. Talia Mae Bettcher conceives of resistant spaces that fulfill this function as "trans worlds" in which trans people can find respite from cisnormative impositions (Bettcher, "Trapped" 389). However, spaces that can function as trans worlds are finite and might be

---

5   Muñoz uses the notion of worldmaking to highlight the "ability" of minoritarian performances "to establish" counterpublics as "alternate views of the world" (*Disidentification* 195). Similarly, I use the term to describe the capacity of trans readers to (re-)appropriate elements from science fiction texts that were not meant to address them or that include harmful elements. I further use the term to show the ways in which trans authors use the genre's conventions to create new trans sf narratives and how trans readers may affectively attach to them as communal resources that transcend the constraints of cisnormative worlds, acting as spaces that validate and reflect their experiences, identities, and struggles through those of the stories' respective characters.

difficult to access or even be entirely out of reach for some of us—particularly for BIPOC, poor, disabled, or otherwise marginalized or rural trans folks.

Trans Worldmaking and Science Fiction

For this reason, I have asserted in my research that cultural and literary narratives can serve a similar function of having our experiences validated and reflected, thereby potentially offering the prospect of a more hopeful future. For, as Judith Butler holds, the realm of fantasy may be "what allows us to imagine ourselves and others otherwise" and transcend and challenge the norms that marginalize us (*Undoing* 29). Hence, (science fiction) narratives may allow for the creation and circulation of and participation in "alternative world[s] in which other forms of identification and social relations become imaginable" (Rodriguez 26).

Therefore, the recent expansion in cultural visibility within North American science fiction stories holds tremendous potential for trans readers. This may be said to be particularly true for trans-authored stories. For, as Gossett, Stanley, and Burton argue: "Immense transformational and liberatory possibilities arise from what are otherwise sites of oppression or violent extraction . . . when individuals have agency in their representation" (xvi). Indeed, trans science fiction stories may serve to create "provisional collectivities" by offering the potential of "new forms of recognition, relation, and community" (Horak, "Visibility" 100). For example, these texts may serve as a foil to help process and share discriminatory experiences and the resulting feelings of pain, shame, and rage. To be sure, seeing our experiences "mirror[ed]" may help to mitigate feelings of isolation and invalidation (Malatino, "Though" 134).

As such, trans science fiction narratives can be seen as an outgrowth and a form of trans utopianism that enables the creation and sharing of hopeful and supportive stories of communality, as well as external communication, that offer "autonomous spaces in which to breathe" (Jones 3). Indeed, as Muñoz asserts, the straight (and I would add cis) present can be made more bearable if it is "known in relation to the alternative temporal and spatial maps provided by a perception of past and future affective worlds" (*Cruising* 27). In fact, witnessing that others also "share a similar crucible" (Malatino, "Though" 135) may help process trauma and (re-)build resilience. Hence, the narratives may produce a sense of communality that aid in their reframing "as a justified response to situations of injustice" (Malatino, "Though" 133). This belief also finds its reflection in Martin Joseph Ponce's observation that "[g]ay and lesbian readers frequently attest to the pivotal role that reading for representations of same-sex desire has played in facilitating sexual self-understanding and alleviating a sense of isolation" (317). Indeed, similar to how Michael Warner describes the power of queer stories, trans science fiction stories may enable trans readers "in isolated places around the country and around the world [to] know, if only vaguely, that somewhere things are different: somewhere they can go and find strangers with whom they can share an intimate world" (qtd. in Jagose, "Queer"). Thus, as Laura Horak observes about YouTube videos by trans creators, they may "tell trans youth that self-determination and transformation are viable routes," as they "solicit desire, empathy, and emulation" ("Visibility" 581), thereby creating a sense of community and be/longing (582).

Hence, these narratives may function as affective communal resources, as they constitute opportunities of trans worldmaking in that "trans subjects may reach out to [...them] as a surface for becoming" (Keegan, "Revisitation" 30),[6] thus allowing for "[re-]negotiation[s] of the terms of selfhood and belonging" (Drabinski 305). Michael Warner has discussed this potentially supportive role of textual encounters as worldmaking practices under the heading of counterpublics. Warner defines counterpublics as "multicontextual spaces of circulation, organized not by a place or an institution but by the circulation of discourse" ("Publics" 85). As Rita Felski notes, narratives may fulfill this function

---

6   While Keegan talks about the possibilities of "[a]esthetic transgendering" ("Revisitation" 30) of narratives that do not explicitly depict trans representation, I feel that this argument also applies to more overt and direct forms of recognition ("Revisitation" 26–27; 30).

of acting "as lifelines for those deprived of other forms of public acknowledgment" in the face of "patent asymmetry and unevenness of
structures of recognition" (*Uses* 43).[7]

Claudia Breger has discussed this potential under the heading of
"affective narrative worldmaking" ("Configuration" 241). According to
Breger, narrative worldmaking entails the exchange of "affects, associations, attention, experiences, evaluations, forms, matter, perspectives,
perceptions, senses, sense, topoi and tropes in and through specific
media" ("Configuration" 242). Breger argues that readers "orient" themselves in relation to the text by "performing comparisons" and through
"associations" with previous affective experiences, textual encounters,
and their own historically and socially situated positionalities ("Narratology" 245). Consequently, processes of affective worldmaking are
characterized by a complex, spontaneous, and unpredictable intermin-
gling of elements of texts and our "lifeworld experiences," and their associated affects that hold the potential to "(re-)configur[e]" both our relationship to texts (Breger, "Configuration" 244; 231), but, as I suggest,
also to ourselves, our lives, and others.

Here, the affective charge of the stories I have discussed becomes
essential. For, as Silvia Schultermandl suggests, the readers may "feel[]
connected to an unknown reading public based on the understanding
that what unites them is their experience of the affective structures a
text evokes" (253). In fact, Schultermandl finds that these "feeling[s] of
kinship" are the result of readers "becom[ing] part of the text," as they
"invest" their "own ideas[,]" experiences, and emotions "into the text"
(260). They fulfill a longing for a world or worlds in which our identities are not only seen and tolerated but believed, accepted, affirmed,
celebrated, and reflected in those of other trans people. As such, they
stand in opposition to and suggest alternatives to dominant societal
structures that invalidate our identities and may even threaten our very

---

7   Felski includes this capacity for offering moments of recognition alongside en-
     chantment, knowledge, and shock as the four "modes of textual engagement"
     (*Uses* 14).

existence. Thus, these alternative trans-oriented discourses act as counterpublics that potentially offer points of recognition and hope to trans folks. For, as Lauren Berlant suggests, "a tiny point of identification can open up a field of fantasy and de-isolation, of vague continuity, or of ambivalence" (*Female* 11). Indeed, the affective charge and often everydayness of the narratives I have discussed are productive in this way, as they may invite feelings of communality (Felski, *Beyond* 94), which "seems to emanate from" a shared sense of "history" between readers, texts, characters, narrators, and authors and "their ongoing attachments and actions" (Berlant, *Female* 5).

Moreover, these stories may suggest blueprints for more accepting and validating social relations, trans be/longing, and trans for trans (t4t) care,[8] as well as the promise of more affirming and broader social worlds (Bettcher, "Trapped" 389). For, as Felski highlights, recognition in reading and representation can bring about both "moment[s] of personal illumination and heightened self-understanding" and "practices of acknowledgment" as well as "acceptance and validation" in the wider social and political realm (*Uses* 30).

Potential Limits of Trans Worldmaking

While Laura Horak maintains that trans "visibility" may function both as an assertion of "trans people's existence and humanity" and as "a form of collective worldmaking and radical imagination" ("Vulnerability" 98), this does not mean that this potential is universal, guaranteed, or necessarily unproblematic. In fact, as Nancy Fraser shows, although subaltern counterpublics might aid in "expand[ing] discursive space," they can be marked by "their own modes of informal exclusion and

---

8   Hil Malatino conceives of "trans for trans (t4t)" care as a praxis of "creative and caring acts of trans intimacy that render life in the interregnum—in the moments during transition . . .—not only livable but also, sometimes joyous" ("Future" 635).

marginalization" (67). In other words, potential moments of affirmation and recognition may not be actualized in the same manner, as they emerge through the interplay between the respective texts and potential readers. Therefore, a particular text's potential for recognition may vary according to the individual reader's positionality. For, as Che Gosset points out, trans visibility is often "premised on invisibility" in that, in order to "bring a select few into view," it tends to make other less desirable subjects "disappear into the background" and thus "reinforces oppression" (1831–84). Therefore, the increased visibility and the extent to which they may be said to hold transformative potential may be determined by the diversity of voices and perspectives within trans-authored science fiction and the representations it generates.

Moreover, moments of recognition may not only be reassuring or empowering. They may also be uncanny, uncomfortable, disconcerting, disruptive, and even (re-)traumatizing (Felski, *Uses* 29). Hence, these texts can also be difficult for trans readers to read since they might feel triggering and too close to home (cf. Nuttall 393)—rather than serving as "an escape or release from one's everyday existence" (Felski, *Uses* 34–35).[9] For example, in researching these texts for my dissertation, I found that I often needed a break after reading a narrative that reminded me of some of my own painful experiences. [10]

Thus, stories like Nino Cipri's "The Shape of My Name," in which the narrator uses letters and time travel, in an attempt to gain his absent mother's recognition, and Jeanne Thornton's "The L7 Gene" that explores familial rejection through the allegory of a narrator coming home for Thanksgiving only to learn that her mother created a cisgender clone of

---

9   In fact, Suzanne Keen suggests that "[e]xtreme personal distress in response to narrative usually interrupts and sometimes terminates the narrative transaction" (Keen, "Narrative").

10   As Felski notes, moments of recognition in literary works can be "[s]imultaneously reassuring and unnerving," as they "bring[] together likeness and difference in one fell swoop" (Felski, *Uses* 25). As a result, recognizing oneself may also be troubling in that it might even "inspire[] a revised or altered sense of who [... we are]" (Felski, *Uses* 25), that might "not always [be] flatter[ing]" (Felski, *Uses* 48).

her pretransition self, hit home particularly hard. On the other hand, narratives like Susan Jane Bigelow's "The Heart's Cartography" and RJ Edwards' "What Cheer," whose narrators find recognition, (self-)acceptance, and hope in the friendship with a time traveler or in the companionship of a visiting alien that takes on their appearance to "walk" with them, felt reaffirming and reinvigorating. Finally, Julian K. Jarboe's "The Heavy Things"[11] and Gillian Ybabez's "Lisa's Story: Zombie Apocalypse"[12] brought to mind my own frustrations, fears, and struggles with navigating cisnormative environments and medical systems in which recognition, support, personal autonomy, self-determination, and safety are all too often conditional and precarious—even if I do not always share all of the characters' experiences.

However, even seemingly optimistic or utopian narratives may not just result in positive affective experiences. They may also trigger feelings "of envy, annoyance, jealousy, . . . judgment[,]" and of missing out that are themselves the result of "survival struggles" in cisnormative worlds in which trans acceptance, or even safety, remains scarce and fragile (Malatino, "Future" 656). Consequently, trans worldmaking may be said to be both a promising and complicated praxis of trans for trans care (t4t) since, according to Malatino, one "can't presuppose or predicate such love on identitarian or subjective sameness" ("Future" 656). Nonetheless, the proliferation of trans-authored and themed science fiction narratives may hold tremendous "formative and transformative power," as it allows us to craft and share self-determined stories about our identities, experiences, and worlds (Gossett et al. xvii). As such, it can open up new possibilities for affective connections and support through trans worldmaking in the face of an all-too-often devastatingly transphobic present (Gossett, et al. xvi–xvii; cf. Muñoz, *Cruising* 27).

---

11   Jarboe's story offers a powerful and visceral portrayal of its narrator's bodily dysphoria that is ultimately exacerbated when they are deprived of their agency and access to medical care.

12   Gillian Ybabez's story, "Lisa's Story: Zombie Apocalypse," explores the themes of discrimination and violence faced by trans people—particularly black and trans women of color—through the lens of a zombie apocalypse.

This is particularly true when this new subgenre of science fiction fulfills its potential for diversifying voices and perspectives, be it in terms of authorship, characters, or experiences.

Bibliography

Berlant, Lauren. *The Female Complaint: The Unfinished Business of Sentimentality in American Culture*. Duke UP, 2008.

Bettcher, Talia Mae. "Trapped in the Wrong Theory: Rethinking Trans Oppression and Resistance." *Signs: Journal of Women in Culture and Society*, vol. 39, no. 2, 2014, pp. 383–406.

Bigelow, Susan Jane. "The Heart's Cartography." *Transcendent 3: The Year's Best Transgender Speculative Fiction*, edited by Bogi Takács, Lethe Press, 2018, pp. 229–241.

Breger, Claudia. "Affect and Narratology." *The Palgrave Handbook of Affect Studies and Textual Criticism*, edited by Thomas Blake and Donald R. Wehrs, Palgrave Macmillan, 2017, pp. 235–57.

——. "Affects in Configuration: A New Approach to Narrative Worldmaking." *Narrative*, vol. 25, no. 2, 2017, pp. 227–51.

Butler, Judith. *Undoing Gender*. Routledge, 2004.

Cipri, Nino. "The Shape of My Name." *Transcendent: The Year's Best Transgender Speculative Fiction*, edited by K. M Szpara, 2016, pp. 1–16.

Crawford, Lucas. "A Transgender Poetics of the High Line Park." *TSQ: Transgender Studies Quarterly*, vol. 1, no. 4, Jan. 2014, pp. 482–500.

Drabinski, Kate. "'Incarnate Possibilities: Female to Male Transgender Narratives and the Making of Self.'" *Journal of Narrative Theory*, vol. 44, no. 2, 2014, pp. 304–29.

Earl, Jessie. *Star Trek's Accidental Transgender Episode*. 2018, https://www.youtube.com/watch?v=PQoxKWGU6b8.

Edwards, RJ. "What Cheer." *Meanwhile, Elsewhere: Science Fiction and Fantasy from Transgender Writers*, edited by Cat Fitzpatrick and Casey Plett, Topside Press, 2017, pp. 30–52.

Felski, Rita. *Beyond Feminist Aesthetics: Feminist Literature and Social Change*. Harvard UP, 1989.

——. *Uses of Literature*. Blackwell Pub, 2008.

Fraser, Nancy. "Rethinking the Public Sphere: A Contribution to the Critique of Actually Existing Democracy." *Social Text*, no. 25/26, 1990, pp. 56–80.

Gossett, Che. "Blackness and the Trouble of Trans Visibility." *Trap Door: Trans Cultural Production and the Politics of Visibility*, edited by Reina Gossett et al., The MIT Press, 2017, pp. 183–90.

Gossett, Reina, et al. "Known Unknowns: An Introduction to Trap Door." *Trap Door: Trans Cultural Production and the Politics of Visibility*, edited by Reina Gossett et al., The MIT Press, 2017, pp. xv–xxvi.

hooks, bell. *Talking Back: Thinking Feminist, Thinking Black*, new edition, Routledge, 2015.

Horak, Laura. "Trans on YouTube: Intimacy, Visibility, Temporality." *TSQ: Transgender Studies Quarterly*, vol. 1, no. 4, Jan. 2014, pp. 572–85.

——. "Visibility and Vulnerability." *The Power of Vulnerability*, edited by Anu Koivunen et al., Manchester University Press, 2018, pp. 95–115.

Jagose, Annamarie. "Queer World Making: Annamarie Jagose Interviews Michael Warner." *Genders*, 1 May 2000, https://www.colorado.edu/gendersarchive19982013/20-00/05/01/queer-world-makingannamarie-jagose-interviews-michael-warne. Genders 1998–2013.

Jarboe, Julian K. "The Heavy Things." *Transcendent 3: The Year's Best Transgender Speculative Fiction*, edited by Bogi Takács, Lethe Press, 2018, pp. 193–95.

Jones, Angela. "Introduction: Queer Utopias, Queer Futurity, and Potentiality in Quotidian Practice." *A Critical Inquiry into Queer Utopias*, edited by Angela Jones, Palgrave Macmillan, 2013, pp. 1–17, http://site.ebrary.com/id/10775602.

Keegan, Cael M. "Revisitation: A Trans Phenomenology of the Media Image." *MedieKultur: Journal of Media and Communication Research*, vol. 32, no. 61, Dec. 2016, pp. 26–41.

Keen, Suzanne. "Narrative Empathy." *The Living Handbook of Narratology*, edited by Jan Christoph Meister et al., Hamburg University, 2013, http://www.lhn.uni-hamburg.de/node/42.html.

Lothian, Alexis. "Feminist and Queer Science Fiction in America." *The Cambridge Companion to American Science Fiction*, edited by Eric Carl Link and Gerry Canavan, Cambridge UP, 2015, pp. 70–82.

Malatino, Hil. "Future Fatigue." *TSQ: Transgender Studies Quarterly*, vol. 6, no. 4, Nov. 2019, pp. 635–58.

——. "Tough Breaks: Trans Rage and the Cultivation of Resilience." *Hypatia*, vol. 34, no. 1, 2019, pp. 121–40.

Melzer, Patricia. "Sexuality." *The Oxford Handbook of Science Fiction*, edited by Rob Latham, Oxford UP, 2014, pp. 395–407.

Morgan, Cheryl. "Tipping the Fantastic: How the Transgender Tipping Point Has Influenced Speculative Fiction." *Gender Identity and Sexuality in Current Fantasy and Science Fiction*, edited by F. T Barbini, 2017, pp. 83–103.

Muñoz, José Esteban. *Cruising Utopia: The Then and There of Queer Futurity*. New York UP, 2009.

——. *Disidentifications: Queers of Color and the Performance of Politics*. University of Minnesota Press, 1999.

Nicolazzo, Z., et al. "An Exploration of Trans* Kinship as a Strategy for Student Success." *International Journal of Qualitative Studies in Education*, vol. 30, no. 3, Mar. 2017, pp. 305–19.

Nuttall, Sarah. "Reading, Recognition and the Postcolonial." *Interventions*, vol. 3, no. 3, Jan. 2001, pp. 391–404.

Ponce, Martin Joseph. "Queers Read What Now?" *GLQ: A Journal of Lesbian and Gay Studies*, vol. 24, no. 2–3, June 2018, pp. 315–41.

Rodriguez, Juana Maria. *Sexual Futures, Queer Gestures, and Other Latina Longings*. New York UP, 2014.

Schultermandl, Silvia. "Reading for Connectivity: Aesthetics and Affect in Intermedial Autobiographies 2.0." *Interactions: Studies in Communication & Culture*, vol. 9, no. 2, July 2018, pp. 251–63.

Wallace, Belinda Deneen. "Queer Potentialities and Queering Home in Shani Mootoo's Cereus Blooms at Night." *Cultural Dynamics*, vol. 30, no. 1–2, Feb. 2018, pp. 59–75.

Warner, Michael. "Publics and Counterpublics." *Public Culture*, vol. 14, no. 1, 2002, pp. 49–90.

Whybrew, Si Sophie Pages. "Transgender and Nonbinary Trek Characters." *Routledge Handbook to Star Trek*, edited by Leimar Garcia-Siino et al., Routledge, 2021. Forthcoming.

Ybabez, Gillian. "Lisa's Story: Zombie Apocalypse." *Transcendent 2: The Year's Best Transgender Speculative Fiction*, edited by Bogi Takács, Lethe Press, 2017, pp. 111–119.

Labor of Love and Other Stories: Post-Yugoslav Feminist Narratives and Art-based Practices

Jelena Petrović

Love has become a visible political issue since the October Revolution, especially when it comes to women's emancipation and social reproduction.[1] The ideology of egalitarian social relations, common ownership of the means of production, and, above all, the liberation from all hegemonic forms of human oppression resulted in a certain amount of progress in the fields of sexuality, morality, and love, at least for a while. However, this progress was by no means radical enough to instigate changes in the material conditions of social reproduction, and the nuclear family survived after the revolution as the basic social unit and the ultimate outcome of love relationships. New social ideas of free or red love that required a radical change of material practices failed to be realized, despite the hopeful prospects offered by communism at the time. Following the new social imagination of free love, the avant-garde literature in the wake of World War I called for a new approach to the old topics, a new language, and a new people who would be freed from moral prejudices and conservative or patriarchal conventions. In the spirit of the European modernist movements that emerged during and after WWI, the Yugoslav avant-garde challenged many women

1   Research for this chapter was partly conducted under the FWF Elise Richter project, entitled *The Politics of Belonging. Art Geographies*, supported by the Austrian Science Fund (FWF No. V730).

authors to resort to an emancipatory politics of love and its socially engaged struggle. One of the crucial interventions of interwar Yugoslav women's authorship was achieved precisely through those literary narratives that liberate love from the socially pre-constructed concepts of gender. This, in turn, opened up new possibilities for the interpretation of love in an emancipatory context.[2]

Furthermore, this new paradigm of free love introduced by the October Revolution spread throughout different women's movements and feminist networks, thus becoming an integral part of women's emancipation in interwar Yugoslavia. Articles about women's struggles, feminism, the rise of communism, and socialism from the October Revolution to the Spanish Civil War, as well as from Africa, Asia, America, and Australia, became regular contributions to Yugoslav interwar women's journals, such as: *Ženski svijet* (Women's World, Zagreb), *Ženski list* (Women's Gazette) and *Naša žena* (Our Women, Ljubljana), *Žena danas* (Women Today, Belgrade) and others (Petrović, *The Women's Authorship*). Following the red thread of the same ideological struggle, during World War II, the journal *Žena danas* (Women Today) became the "legal" voice of the largest Yugoslav women's movement, Anitfašistički front žena (Women's Antifascist Front, abbrev. AFŽ). After WWII, this journal was continually published until 1981 and dealt with the social, cultural, and literary engagement of women in socialist Yugoslavia, but unfortunately, this time in a less progressive way, at least regarding the further emancipation of women in the new socialist, but still patriarchal society.

The revolutionary understanding of red or free love formed the basis for utopian ideas of fellowship and community that ultimately contributed to the resistance against the mechanisms of human and espe-

---

2   The idea of *red love* can be traced through many novels as one of the main subjects of the feminist writing in interwar Yugoslavia, to mention just a few: Sofka Kveder's *Hanka* (1917), Marijana Kokalj Željeznova's *Brezdomci* (1930, The Homeless), Julka Hlapec Đorđević's *Jedno dopisivanje—fragmenti romana* (1932, A Correspondence—Fragments of a Novel). See Petrović, *The Women's Authorship*.

cially women's exploitation that followed the October Revolution. Still, it may be argued that the repudiation of the idea of red love reflected the remnants of patriarchal, capitalist, and colonial power relations after the revolution, even if they were not always obvious during socialism. In any case, the question of labor and love, i.e., of their mutual relationship and delimitation, has remained unsolved and marginalized to this day. Nonetheless, it continues to be essential, particularly for those who continue to dream of and fight for a better egalitarian world.

Especially during the last decade, many writers, curators, theorists, and activists—and often all at once—opened a new chapter in feminist art and work, anchored in the post-Yugoslav context, that deals with the relationship between love and social emancipation, love and revolution, and, finally, between love and labor. With reference to previous revolutionary struggles, particularly to the emancipatory heritage of Yugoslav socialism, these new feminist endeavors drew attention to a singular definition of women's liberation and its understanding of red feminism.[3] Today, these post-Yugoslav individual, collaborative, and collective feminist art practices point to how the politics of red love and leftist thought have survived, despite the brutal impact of historical revisionism on the (post-)war and post-socialist society.

In order to explore the meaning of red or free love today, this text follows a few paradigmatic examples of feminist art-based research

---

3   This definition of *red feminism* unites the Yugoslav socialist legacy of women's antifascist struggle with all the progressive feminist ideas that did not materialize through the emancipation of women in the 20th century and represents the red thread of a unifying, singular movement for the future emancipation of women and society in general in the post-Yugoslav space and elsewhere. The singular definition of women's liberation and its red feminism lies beyond theoretical thinking about the limits and promises of a social utopia, as well as beyond aesthetic questions concerning non-presentable universality of great events and their images; it defines creative processes and practices that involve excess/resistance, freedom, and a yet non-existing political as well as a social singularity that has the potential to create a future beyond the multiple classes and identities in today's neoliberal, patriarchal, and colonial reality (Petrović, "What Does the Freedom Stand for Today?").

and/or performative practices from the post-Yugoslav space:[4] Olga Dimitrijević's play *Crvena ljubav* (2016, Red Love); CRVENA's *Arhiv antifašističke borbe žena Bosne i Hercegovine i Jugoslavije* (2014 ongoing, Archive of Antifascist Struggle of Women of Bosnia and Herzegovina and Yugoslavia) and Andreja Dugandžić and Adela Jušić's public artistic action *Rad ljubavi* (2014, Labour of Love). Reviving the crucial links between the politics of love and emancipation, struggle and labor, from the October Revolution to present day, this paper uses these examples to show that the red revolution is still unfinished for women rather than lost.

The Politics of Red Love

It is important to emphasize that the idea of red love is primarily a reflection of the women's struggle within the October Revolution. In her early political writings, the Russian writer and revolutionary Alexandra Kollontai underlines that the abolishment of private ownership in love relationships, primarily in relation to women and their roles therein, was connected to the abolition of private ownership of the means of production within relations of production. In 1916, this argument was taken a step further by another revolutionary, Inessa Armand, who proposed that the idea of free love should be developed and politically articulated as a revolutionary demand. The correspondence between the two lovers, Inessa Armand and Lenin, about an ideological pamphlet that was to define the role of women in communist society, demonstrated that the revolution was not yet ready to do away with patriarchy

---

4   Like numerous *post-isms*, the term *post-Yugoslav* appears as a means of both historical and political continuation of Yugoslav feminism as well as of the Yugoslav left. It is necessary to clarify the meaning of the paradigm *Yugoslav*, which, in the contemporary context, cannot be discussed unless it is determined as a social signifier, not in the etatistic but in the political sense of what Yugoslavia as an abolished revolutionary subject represents today, particularly in relation to the war process of its "abolishment" in the 1990s (Petrovic, "What is Left of the Feminist Left?").

and its institutions—marriage and family. In one of his letters, Lenin pronounced Armand's proposition to be inconceivable, as it was supposedly based on her personal wishes rather than on any objective class relations anchored in the social circumstances of the times. To counter her position that even minor infatuation and intimacy are more poetic and purer than loveless kisses in some vulgar and shallow conjugal relationship, he proposes a series of questions that support his belief that bourgeois marriage has to be replaced with civil marriage founded on love and respect, but that marriage as an institution is a necessity within the new social order. Believing the idea of free love to be absurd, politically wrong, and more bourgeois than proletarian, Lenin discredits such comparison as illogical, as these situations are, in his view, incomparable (Lenin 182–185). Although they were never fully realized, the social and ideological endeavors by Alexandra Kollontai and her female political comrades, such as Inessa Armand, foregrounded the problem in the new revolutionary society's understanding of love and sexuality, as well as social morals, at the turn of the 20th century. The idea of red love came to life more in political and literary writings than in the communist reality of the time. Their experiences demonstrated the degree to which gender and class remained (un)considered within revolutionary ideas. Additionally, they revealed that economic and ideological relations are inseparable when it comes to women's struggle for an emancipated or red love.

Almost a century later, Olga Dimitrijević's play *Crvena ljubav* (Red Love), performed for the first time in Belgrade's Bitef Theatre in February 2016, brought this radical idea of love from the October Revolution to the stage. Following the plot of Kollontai's novel *Vasilisa Malygina* (1923, Red Love, 1927), Dimitrijević portrays the love relationship of Vasilisa and Vladimir, who met during the revolution as passionate idealists, focusing on their social and political lives within the community. Five years later, Vasilisa remains loyal to her revolutionary ideals. Vladimir, on the other hand, has betrayed not only his principles but also his relationship with Vasilisa by using all the privileges of his executive position. But still, in the end, Dimitrijević leaves hope that the next (women's) revolution will change the world—making the idea of red love a reality.[5] Through its main characters, this love becomes a unifying element that represents an essential social emotion for any collective or community in the new free world. Here, liberated from any kind of institutional or class oppression, primarily the institutions of marriage and bourgeois family, the idea of red love is presented as a profound social emotion, rather than a private matter between two persons in love (Kollontai 278–279).

Accordingly, Olga Dimitrijević reworked the revolutionary idea of love during the socialist revolution to show both its victories and defeats. By connecting the time of the October Revolution with the past of socialist Yugoslavia, the play creates the same sense of a lost struggle, by sharing the fact that patriarchy has resisted every leftist revolution to this day. Therefore, this *red love* points to the repetitive history of today's struggle for free love that has not yet been won. Despite some glorious moments of women's liberation in the socialist past, red love has remained an unrealized dream on the revolutionary road to the full emancipation from patriarchal and other overpowering mechanisms of social and political oppression, not only in the (post-)Yugoslav space but also beyond.

The Politics of Love and Struggle

Apart from free love, which was simultaneously propagated and suppressed by the October Revolution, the question of women's invisible labor, in the wake of many socialist revolutions following WWII, challenged the concepts of love and family. Despite being largely unknown internationally, the Yugoslav example of the Women's Antifascist Front (AFŽ, 1942–1953) is perhaps one of the largest women's movements that systematically focused on the economic aspects of reproductive and domestic labor during the socialist period from the 1940s onwards. Nowa-

---

5   Here, Olga Dimitrijević utilizes one of the most famous Yugoslav chansons of Beti Đorđević: *Počnimo ljubav iz početka* (1976, Let's start our love from the beginning).

days, the increasingly rediscovered and systematized archives show that
the ideas originating from the AFŽ continue to be highly relevant and
radical with respect to the organization of women's everyday lives, their
social relations, and their new socialist roles. Thus, efforts to archive,
digitalize, and systematize the AFŽ legacy have become especially relevant in recent years.

The largest AFŽ archive was initiated, designed, and digitized by
members of the Association for Culture and Art—CRVENA, based in
Sarajevo.[6] The idea behind this archive started in 2010 at CRVENA's
8th of March initiative *Živi solidarnost!* (Live Solidarity!) and continued
through different research and artistic activities, events, and actions
under the slogan: "What has our struggle given us?" In 2014, artists,
researchers, and feminists Andreja Dugandžić and Adela Jušić began
the work of creating a systematic digital archive of thousands of documents, photographs, secondary sources, and works of art connected
to the history of the AFŽ that had been forgotten and neglected after
the collapse of Yugoslav socialism. On the occasion of the 8th of March
2015, the online Archive of Antifascist Struggle of Women of Bosnia and
Herzegovina and Yugoslavia (abbrev. AFŽ archive)[7] was launched by CR-
VENA. Following this, in 2016, the AFŽ archive published a book titled
Izgubljena revolucija: Antifašistički front žena između mita i stvarnosti (Lost
Revolution: Women's Anti-Fascist Front Between Myth and Forgetting)
to contribute to and advance the research of this singular Yugoslav example of women's revolutionary struggle. Dealing with the revolution
that marked a historical turning point for Yugoslav women, this collaborative volume critically and analytically discusses the history, lessons,
and accomplishments of these women's struggles, or more precisely,
the ruptures and contradictions of their revolutionary past. As an impulse for future research, artworks, and exhibitions, this archive not

---

6   Focusing on the relation between feminism, Yugoslav history, and contempo-
     rary art, *Crvena* was founded in 2010 by a group of friends who created this com-
     mon space to deal with the politics of everyday life from different artistic, cu-
     ratorial, activist, theoretical, and other backgrounds (www.crvena.ba).

7   The AFŽ archive is fully available on www.afzarhiv.org.

only made visible a huge part of the marginalized history of Yugoslav women but also brought it back to life.[8]

The AFŽ archive can also be taken as a testament to how patriarchal structures survived after WWII under the auspices of new socialist gender roles. These new gender roles, within which the responsibility for care and (the labor of) love were exclusively assigned to women, were made possible by the patriarchal patterns internalized and hidden by socialism. As a result, the AFŽ was (self-)abolished in 1953, under the pretext that it was no longer necessary, as the woman question had already been solved, according to the Communist Party of Yugoslavia. Despite the efforts of Yugoslav women at the time, the battle against patriarchy was lost in the early period of Yugoslav socialism. Immediately after the abolition of the AFŽ, Mitra Mitrović, one of the founders and leaders of the AFŽ movement during and after WWII, observed with resignation that the woman question was shut down without justification right at the moment when it was finally beginning to be resolved. Indeed, according to her, the exploitation of women originated from their closest and most loved ones:

> But it seems that in this question, perhaps more than in the case of racial or class issues, the enslavement is less disguised and more complex, because it does not depend solely on those who hold the power, those who are distant and foreign, rich and white, but also on the closest people, individuals such as father and brother, son even, who cannot themselves overcome the prejudice and beliefs that were imposed

---

8   In addition to individual and collaborative events, artworks, and exhibitions emerging from this digitized online archive, the exhibition *Polet žena* (Verve of Women) was installed as a permanent collection in December 2019 after months-long research of the AFŽ materials in the Historical Museum of Bosnia and Herzegovina in Sarajevo. Consisting of numerous artifacts from the museum's holdings, archival documents, photographs, books, periodicals, posters, and three-dimensional objects, the exhibition was curated by one of the initiators of the AFŽ archive, Andreja Dugandžić, in collaboration with CRVENA's members and became a permanent part of the museum. The design of the exhibition was done by visual artist Lala Rašćić with reference to the modernist Yugoslav design of the museum.

upon them—a long time ago, yes, but which have nevertheless become constituent parts of life, customs, and house rules. (Mitrović 5)

The struggle for women's emancipation during socialism continued for
a while after the AFŽ ceased to exist. Vida Tomšič, the last leader of the
AFŽ as well as one of the few women who remained politically powerful until the end of socialism in Yugoslavia, insisted on the transformation of the woman question into a so-called universal struggle for
women's emancipation that should be primarily based on the policy of
care (Tomšič, *O zakonski zvezi, družini in gospodinjstvu v socializmu*). The
main task of this policy was to resolve the conflicting double burden of
women's roles in 'work' (employment) and 'care' (housework). Within
this new socialist society, marriage and romantic relationships were
defined as a civil category based on true love and mutual understanding between equal partners (as defined by Lenin earlier in the text).
This new paradigm of love changed pre-socialist conservative conceptions of family, personal relationships, and marriage. Thus, it promised
free choice of partner, divorce, property sharing, remarriage, etc. At the
same time, it rejected free love as a pseudo-revolutionary, amoral, and
dangerous matter that affected women in particular. Vida Tomšič often
cited the program of the League of Communists of Yugoslavia to warn
so-called "ultra-revolutionaries" that free or red love was unacceptable
to Yugoslav society:

> At the ideological and political level, the Communists are leading and
> will lead the fight against those ridiculous ideological and moral con-
> ceptions which, under the pseudo-revolutionary phrase of destroying
> class morality, in fact, propagate immorality in relations between the
> sexes. (Tomšič, *Žena u razvoju socijalstičke samoupravne Jugoslavije* 64)

By including various women's writings and historical documents from
the late 1950s onwards, the AFŽ archive reveals that the process of universal transformation of society was defined by the socialist self-man-
agement system in which women participated in significantly fewer
numbers than in the AFŽ. This system aimed at the communization
of family life and the modernization of partnerships through a new di-

vision of labor between man and woman. This meant establishing new institutional support for the household and motherhood, increasing the economic independence of women, and building socialist residential areas that would meet the needs of new social communities based on gender equality. During that time, the concept of functional and socially responsible architecture primarily focused on the social problem of childcare and housework. As such, it brought some great ideas that were implemented through common kitchens, kindergartens, washing-houses, and other shared spaces of new urban communities. However, housework and motherhood were mainly viewed as women's labor of love.

Although it seemed that socialism would bring about gender equality and change gender roles with regards to labor, leisure, and (im)possible relationships, it did not. In fact, the classless society, in which all issues of inequality under capitalism or any other circumstances should have been resolved, was all too eager to internalize patriarchy through gender roles when it came to both labor and love.

Labor of Love

A few decades later, the problems of reproductive labor, romanticizing the exploitation of women and normalizing heteropatriarchal notions of sexuality and love, became part of a new women's and feminist struggle under the somewhat different circumstances of capitalism. In the 1970s, criticism of the labor of love reframed sexual, love, and romantic relationships as labor relations and thus gave impetus to the international *Wages for Housework Campaign*, initiated in Italy in 1972. Among other things, the Marxist feminists demanded that the questions of gender roles and reproductive labor be resolved; that women should be allowed to work outside their homes; that they should receive unemployment benefits; that they should have equal salaries and be entitled to pregnancy leave; and that all those social formations that were based on gender roles, desires, and the redistribution of leisure time, reflecting gender inequality, should be changed. Many Western Marxist feminists framed reproductive labor as unpaid productive work that women unconditionally perform as a labor of love. Consequently, like the AFŽ in Yugoslavia, they saw the conditions of unconditional and invaluable love as nothing more than a romanticized version of the exploitation of women, within which unpaid, invisible, affective, reproductive, or domestic labor could be perpetuated with impunity.

Inspired by Mariarosa Dalla Costa, Selma James, and Silvia Federici, the co-founders of the *Wages for Housework Movement*, Andreja Dugandžić and Adela Jušić performed the public artistic action *Rad ljubavi* (2014, Labour of Love) a few decades later.[9] Making public the political struggle for the denaturalization of women's unacknowledged labor, this performance is also reminiscent of the emancipatory achievements of women in the Yugoslav past, some of which had been lost in the meantime. Dealing with the issue of women's unpaid, flexible, and invisible labor in the (post-)Yugoslav space, these two artists intervened by using sprays and acrylic colors to create a public collage of images and texts from the Yugoslav educational publications on home economics. The black and white print outside the Historical Museum of Bosnia and Herzegovina in Sarajevo (measuring about 45 square meters) was used as a public surface for well-known Marxist feminist statements about women's reproductive and domestic work. This public performance re-articulates not only the 1970s Marxist feminist thoughts about motherhood and housework but also unpaid labor, domestic violence, and family care. It directly points to women's exploitation for the benefit of the brutal transition to capitalist accumulation in the post-Yugoslav space during and after the 1990s war(s).

Over time, through historical narratives of feminist resistance, this collaborative work also restores sexuality as an important political issue of women's social lives. As such, it focuses on re-centering the politics

---

9   Realized for the first time within CRVENA's exhibition *Moja kuća je i tvoja kuća* (My house is your house, too), curated by Danijela Dugandžić, this print and graffiti artistic action, entitled *Rad ljubavi* (Labour of Love), was repeated in different contexts and traveled the world in various exhibitions.

of desire and sexual freedom, which are essential in defining today's women's struggle for an egalitarian and emancipated life. Accordingly, Dugandžić and Jušić, through a range of public feminist statements, emphasize, among other things, the following:

> Systemic attack on women is directed towards their entire being as well as their sexuality. Within the patriarchal and capitalist frame-work, female sexuality is reduced to passivity, receptivity, sublima-tion, and almost resistance to her own sexual needs. Sexuality is in the service of capitalistic objectives, which consider functions of the uterus, vagina, and clitoris only in the reproduction of the workforce. Within an isolated sphere of the home, the woman is an object over which a man expresses dissatisfaction towards the system which ex-ploits him, or over whom he exercises the power that he is deprived of by that very system (Dugandžić and Jušić).

This radical feminist and leftist approach to the relationship between love and sexuality opens an important social and political discussion about women's history in a revolutionary society. In order to revise the 1970s Marxist feminist practice and thought, as this recent example shows, it appears indispensable and essential to salvage precisely this singularity of red love (Nancy 32).

Other Stories

All previous approaches to the issue of love show that feminist criticism and theory, as well as artistic practices, became more demanding and complex over time, as the dialectics of love emerged as a mode of politi-cal struggle. In addition to the critical approach to the relation between labor and love as well as between love and sexuality, an affirmative ap-proach is increasingly developing that highlights the crucial connection between love and revolution, the social and the subjective, the political and the subconscious, the rational and the affective.

On the one hand, Angela Davis—considered one of the most rev-olutionary feminists in the West—believes that love and labor should

Andreja Dugandžić and Adela Jušić Rad ljubavi (Labour of Love), print and graffiti artistic action, realized as part of Moja kuća je i tvoja kuća (My house is your house, too)

Historical Museum of Bosnia and Herzegovina, Sarajevo, 2014

be reclaimed and essentially altered because it is still women who are in possession of the means necessary for the reproduction of society. According to her, women's appropriation of the family—especially regarding black women who constantly encounter violence and racism in the outside world—could create a new counterpublic sphere. For example, anti-racist family units that are not supremacist, capitalist, and heterosexist could liberate a future common society from multiple systemic inequalities (Davis). On the other hand, Kathi Weeks, a contemporary feminist thinker of Marxist orientation, points out the need to separate the concepts of love and labor in order to reach an understanding of the essential meaning of love today. According to Weeks, only love that is based on a logic of political desire immanent to existence could produce the social imagination of (non-)labor and (non-)family in a commonly shared and solidarity-based post-capitalist society. Weeks further claims that only political reorganization/redefinition of (non-) labor, as well as the affective turn towards the transformation of complex relations of power, subjectivity, and emotions, can trigger radical change in society and lead to a revolution that would truly change the social position of women and of all those who are oppressed by capitalism and patriarchy.

There are, of course, many other theories and practices of contemporary feminist thought which resolve, complicate, and interpret the problem of love—with or without labor. Moira Weigel, the author of *Labour of Love: The Invention of Dating*, argues that these Marxist and feminist theories of "labor in love" and "labor of love" from the past need to be revised and modernized, in line with today's ways of loving, working, and living. She claims that putting the equal sign between labor and love in our contemporary world can often lead to misconceptions and a conservative understanding of their mutual relationship, which implies that we do not have an agenda or even the power to shape and change the world while we keep (re)producing it. Love is an emotion that necessitates a community or other forms of collectivity, "even if it's just a primitive communism of two," because this is the only way of not letting love be completely closed off and co-opted by the meanings which are systematically imposed through today's heteropatriarchal and neoliberal mechanisms of social exploitation (Lennard and Weigel).

From the (post-)Yugoslav feminist perspective, based on previous examples, it is apparent that the meaning of love originates in the dialectical process of pushing the existing borders, by means of questioning, feeling, fighting, and imagining, beyond the gap between so-called Western and other less privileged parts of the world. As these examples show, the need to mark the field of love singularly as a means and the goal of social emancipation has survived primarily in this sphere of feminism, particularly those of leftist orientation. In this dialectical process of becoming, certainly love can give shape to a common struggle for its red singularity, politically and socially.[10]

Finally, it is important to stress that, unlike materialist and collectivist visions of the relationships of both (re)production and love, most contemporary and particularly postmodern conceptions of love and sexuality overlook the economic (class) basis of "the emotional and psychological," in favor of the individual and economically untouchable desire.[11] Although many contemporary theories, to which we have more access, can be complementary to the understanding of love and sexuality—and therefore also desire—they are not sufficient for revolutionary change of the everyday lives of women when it comes to love. Neglecting the importance of the woman question, labor, and economy, in relation to love, leads to its de-politicization as well as its mystification and return to the sphere of the private and intimate exploitation of women. In the end, the social process of emancipating love and sexuality is impossible without interrogating love's economic and libidinal complexities and their resultant power relations within the neoliberal state of today's patriarchal and violent world.

Bibliography

Davis, Angela. *Women, Race, and Class.* Women's Press, 1981.

Dugandžić, Andreja and Adela Jušić. *Labour of Love* (artist's statement), 2014, https://adelajusic.wordpress. com/2015/05/09/labour-of-love/. Accessed December 2020.

---

10   The term *red singularity* has been coined to underline the common ground for a range of feminist and Marxist theories, radical artistic practices, and revolutionary events which lead to the singular (being plural) experience of love that contributes to the permanent emancipation of society. For the term singularity, see the previous definition by Jean-Luc Nancy (32).

11   This generally refers to the psychoanalytic, poststructuralist, and identity approaches to love and sexuality, in particular to those outside of feminist thinking.

Kollontai, Alexandra. *Selected Writings of Alexandra Kollontai*, edited and translated by Alix Holt, Norton, 1977.

Lenin, V.I. *Lenin Collected Works*, vol. 35, Progress Publishers, [1976], www.marxists.org/archive/lenin/works/ 1915/jan/24.htm. Accessed December 2020.

Lennard, Natasha and Moira Weigel. *Love. Labor. Lost. The New York Times*, 17 August 2016, www.nytimes.com/2016/08/17/opinion/love-labor-lost.html. Accessed December 2020.

Mitrović, Mitra. *Položaj žene u savremenom svetu* [The Position of Women in the Contemporary World], Narodna knjiga, 1960.

Nancy, Jean-Luc. *Being Singular Plural*. Stanford UP, 2000.

Petrović, Jelena. "What Does the Freedom Stand for Today?" *Border Thinking*, edited by Marina Gržinić, Stenberg press, The Academy of Fine Arts, 2018.

——. "What is Left of the Feminist Left?" *Feminist Critical Interventions. Thinking Heritage, Decolonising, Crossings*, edited by Biljana Kašić et al., Red Athena UP, 2013.

——. *The Women's Authorship in Interwar Yugoslavia: The Politics of War and Struggle*. Palgrave Macmillan, 2018.

The AFŽ archive. The Association for Culture and Art CRVENA, 2014 ongoing, www.afzarhiv.org. Accessed Decembre 2020.

Duganžić, Adreja and Tijana Okić, editors. *The Lost Revolution: Women's Anti-Fascist Front Between Myth and Forgetting*. Association for Culture and Art CRVENA, 2016 (English edition 2018), http://afzarhiv.org/i tems/show/708. Accessed December 2020.

Tomšič, Vida. *O zakonski zvezi, družini in gospodinjstvu v socializmu* [About Marriage, Family and Household in Socialist Yugoslavia]. Cankarjeva založba, 1959.

——. *Žena u razvoju socijalstičke samoupravne Jugoslavije* [Woman in the development of socialist self-managing Yugoslavia]. Jugoslovenska stvarnost, Newspaper and Publishing House, 1981.

Weeks, Kathi. *Down with Love: Feminist Critique and the New Ideologies of Work*. Verso Books. 13 February 2018, www.verso-books.com/blogs/3614-down-with-love-feminist-critique-and-the-new-ideologies-of-work. Accessed December 2020.

Weigel, Moira. *Labour of Love: The Invention of Dating*. Farrar, Straus & Giroux, 2016.

Damir Arsenijević in Conversation with Šejla Šehabović

Translated by Tag McEntegart

Damir: Let's talk about "Plan B," one of the stories in our graphic novel on environmental violence, which I instigated as a collaborative project between you, as the scriptwriter, Marko Gačnik, as the illustrator, and me, as the editor. The graphic novel is entitled *Zemlja—voda—zrak* (2020, Earth—Water—Air) and bears the name of the first platform for environmental humanities in Bosnia and Herzegovina—*zemljavo-dazrak.com*—which enables research and intervention into the nexus of war-time violence, carried out by authoritarian ethnic elites and environmental violence. The graphic novel examines stories that cover the continued destruction of social structures through environmental violence: from factories destroyed and stripped of assets in enforced and corrupt privatization to illegal and clandestine dumping of hazardous waste in communities, leading to illness and death of its members. But this story, "Plan B," is specific in several regards. Tell me in more detail how you conceived of the idea for the story, from your point of view as the writer.

Šejla: The story was born as a direct response to what I feel are the dominant social affects concerning the pollution created by factories in contemporary post-socialist Bosnia and Herzegovina (BiH). One of these affects is grieving for the loss of the factories. Privatization is corrupt and criminal by nature and has caused a whole 'world' to vanish. We are left with nostalgia and a feeling of loss, which is followed by fear. People are afraid to even talk about it. Even when these factories were in production and not privately owned, they produced disease and death. I unpack that nostalgia and fear. I do this through a literary character who is both father and grandfather. Our parents, especially our fathers, are the people who used their labor to express their masculinity, and they were the ones who built socialist Bosnia and Herzegovina. They were in the limelight. Naturally, our female workers were building our socialist homeland, too, but those who took center stage, such as the engineers, directors, the visible managers of the production process, were educated males. Their lives and masculinity, their right to be judged as valuable members of our society, as well as their own abilities, education, and dedication, depended on the era when socialist society was being created. They were aware that they were destroying nature, and at that time, they firmly believed that they could fully compensate for this through their dedication and innovation. They believed that there was no other way to accomplish such a big leap in material, educational, and cultural advancement. Their contribution to society was measured by the increasing number of people with more secure livelihoods and better prospects. In the period of transition into neoliberal capitalism, they lost their power. In reality, just because they are currently in a powerless and weakened position, like the father in the story "Plan B," now we blame them for having let the socially-owned property slip from their grasp.

The engineers admit that mistakes were made, that there was strife over weighing what portion of the natural environment was worth sacrificing for the good of society. During the transition, they were stripped of their power; they resisted using all of the skills at their disposal; but once they realized they could no longer resist, they started to break down. They were no longer important for a society in which so many people had depended on them. It's important to speak about this because there are environmental movements in Bosnia and Herzegovina who despise these former workers, who would legally prosecute them. These workers need the acknowledgment that they acted rationally. We could not have freed women from patriarchy between '45 and '85 by agricultural work, say, by just growing potatoes, for sure. We could not do that. We could not build 100 schools in

100 villages by growing potatoes. That was not possible. These people knew that something would need to be sacrificed in order to achieve a greater goal. What they could not have planned for is that all the fruits of their sacrifice would be handed over to the capitalists during the transition and that all the burden of the damage of this transition would be shouldered by the workers.

Damir: The so-called post-socialist transition—that is the truncated term for the war against socialist Yugoslavia and its invention of so-cially-owned property—carried out by ethnic elites who bring neolib-eral capitalism through war into the former Yugoslav republics—was marked by sacrificing the workers. At the end of our story, a Hindu businessman buys a factory in BiH and extracts profit from it, while the state turns a blind eye. That puts the workers in a position of extreme loneliness.

Šejla: All those who feel aggrieved think it is only they who have suf-fered losses. I think this is the predominant public sentiment, not only amongst the workers in the factories—we all feel like that.

Damir: You are referring to an individualized sense of guilt, in that we are forced to assume this guilt as individuals, yet it is a burden of guilt that is greater than all of us?

Šejla: That is correct. That is why, in the graphic novel, we have a fa-ther justifying himself to his family. We've been convinced it is all our fault. The resistance I previously mentioned came down either to physi-cal sacrifice or suffering in silence. The health of the engineers was com-promised, and after the war, they suffered from heart conditions and high blood pressure and lived in a state of continuous shock, unable to convince themselves that, from now on, this was how life was going to be. From someone who firmly believed that, by sacrificing some parts of nature, society would be helped; that this country could be transformed for the better, having seen that it was possible with your own eyes, now you are forced to undertake the same sacrifice knowing all too well that it will not benefit society. This is a harrowing position to be in. You work hard, but you do not believe in what you are trying to achieve. This is what it was like when the factories restarted after the war in the late 1990s.

Damir: What emerges from this is that there is a hefty price to be paid for suffering in silence. The father says, "I am silent, but the body remembers."

Šejla: There is a price, and they paid the price. He could build the Koksara factory when he was 25 years old. But, as a mature man with a family, as someone who has proven his masculinity by being able to take care of his family and society, with all his knowledge and experience, he was not able to save society from that factory. It was a heavy blow to the core of his being and everything he knew about himself.

Damir: How would you describe your attitude to history in this story? How does the father inscribe his experience in a wider historical frame when he says, "and there is always someone who wants to secure the future on the back of the current workforce"? In what way does the grandfather, as a literary character, relate to history, and how can his personal experience be critically assessed through the 'lens' of this saying?

Šejla: It is important that you have some insight, that you have a wider grasp of history, in order to be able to pass on that kind of message to the next generation. The problem is that the grandfather in this story does not offer his grandchild more than a glimpse of the emotions stirred by the resistance of the past. A wider historical framework is what is necessary. In a narrow historical framework, which comprises the construction of socialist society, the post-socialist transition, and the destruction of the socialist heritage, only one thing can be preserved: the need to fight for mere survival. The attitude of disengagement is what begins to dominate, the same attitude promoted in the media and education, fostering a feeling of provincialism, disconnection from the wider world, a feeling of ruination and disengagement:

we are constantly persuaded that we have to give up. We should not sacrifice our environment for capitalism. That is the truth. However, in building socialism, we have built something else: the feeling of responsibility towards society. The feeling that silence has no place here. Shall we spend the next 100 years talking about the loss and how incapable we are in the face of it, or shall we talk about the possibility of putting all our capacities for social organization and the tradition of resistance to work for us? We cannot use the "dirty" coking coal; there is more harm than good in it. However, we can use our historical knowledge of how to fight successfully and thus contribute to society. This graphic novel was created by a feminist: it is an attempt to grant mercy to our fathers, to those who, in their era, had a chance to build an egalitarian society, who, in many ways, did participate in building it, and yet today, we treat them as if they had little or no experience in the struggle for emancipation. Whereas that is simply not true.

Damir: Your intervention in this story comes across as a sort of rebellion against a binary polarization: the perpetrator—the victim. Is there another viewpoint that could be espoused?

Šejla: There are both perpetrators and victims here, and all of them are capable of rational thinking and of understanding what happened. The victims here aren't completely helpless. Some of the most educated members of our society are victims. These were people who produced so much capital that an entire society was able to be built from the ground up, so much so that several subsequent generations have places to live, healthcare, and free education. When compared to the lives of their mothers, the lives of our mothers have changed beyond recognition and advanced greatly. In one generation, several important emancipatory landmarks became possible, which were not realized in previous attempts at emancipation. Despite all of today's efforts towards the re-traditionalization of BiH, those who want to turn the clock back have not succeeded in abolishing women's right to abortion, let alone women's right to education; for women to be active in politics; for women to take up senior official positions. The roots of those normalized gains for women and society have deep foundations in our socialist society. But those gains came at a price. The price had to be paid. And one part of the price has included the destruction of the natural environment. Today, the people who destroyed nature, the majority of whom were men, are despised. Unlike most of the workers, the engineers could explain the mistakes they made. These are not the people who will say: in order for society to be affluent, we have to exploit nature, we have to extract everything, poison the water—all that matters is that we produce more capital. They would never say that. They all—rationally and scientifically—know how to present their own factory's actions in the best light. They are ready to talk about the mistakes they made during the most productive, most upbeat, and most glorious period of their lives. That does not deserve our contempt. That is what we need to take into account nowadays when we plan, to be able to create a better, kinder society. Society will never move forward if we are not ready to make sacrifices. However, we should have a consensus on what to sacrifice, when, and at what cost. Today we all pretend that social progress can be made without sacrifice. That is not how it happens.

Damir: This story is clearly gendered. This is a dialogue between a grandfather and his grandson. What is transferred to future generations of men?

Šejla: From a woman's and feminist perspective, as the author, I show how knowledge is transferred from one man to another. The story ends with a lyrical moment, stemming from oral mythology, from local tradition. Resistance doesn't mean just digging your heels in—it has to be planned and well thought through. What is it that you believe in, and what are you willing to sacrifice? Being aware that you have a tradition of resistance that you can call on—that is important.

Damir: Is there an element of resistance in the story that is never explicitly communicated but exists as a tacit understanding?

Šejla: Well, there is a memorial to a mythical goat in Tuzla. But it is not a local story that is found only here in our home town. Istria, too, has memorials dedicated to goats because the goats fed Istrians; they are native to that region, and Istria is their natural habitat. They are part of a natural fire-fighting system because they eat bushes that can become fuel for brush fires—fires that can cause huge damage to the natural environment. In Tuzla, it's different. The officials have constantly forbidden the keeping of goats since they damage the environment. On the other hand, the goats have fed people. There is that same impossible contradiction: you are maintaining the very factory that you know is destroying the natural world. Also, people in the past held the same position: I want to keep a goat even if it eats all the forest, but who cares about forests? That type of resistance is rarely spelled out. And this is what it sounds like when you put it into words: I know that you take from me more than I can produce. In America, when the indigenous population was forbidden to hunt buffalos, supposedly to keep nature intact, they prevented the most experienced stewards of that natural environment from using it wisely. In fact, there is a question of ownership here—it is that question that is never spelled out. The history that is not spoken aloud and the history that "they" will never find out. If the forest is mine, my goat can eat it. But when you take the forest away from me and tell me that it is no longer mine, even though it is my birthright, then my goat can still eat that part of the forest which can never be controlled by any authority in the world. So there!

"We need to imagine a new kind of woman": Narrating Identity in Postwar Women's Magazines in Japan, 1945-1955

Jana Aresin

The end of World War II and Japan's surrender initiated a reexamination of various identities: Japan's national identity on the world stage, but also identities of race, class, and gender. Widespread destruction and the delegitimization of power structures, followed by social, political, and economic reforms that developed in unequal, yet complex, exchanges between the Allied occupation forces, local political elites, and popular organizations, disrupted and called for a redefinition of social and political relations (Miller 5–6; 39–40). Even though these changes were rarely complete, and some only temporary and quickly reversed, the occupation period can still be considered a decisive moment of uncertainty and possibility that marked the transition from imperial Japan to a democratic capitalist US-ally in the Cold War (Dower 23–24). Therefore, it is productive to examine this moment of transition to understand which social and political changes were initiated, delayed, or stifled and which political and ideological dynamics were responsible for them.

One of the social relations challenged during the occupation period were gender relations, along with the appropriate roles and responsibilities of men and women in the 'new democratic Japan' which the occupation forces planned to construct out of the ruins of the war-torn country (Koikari 20–22). In this essay, I analyze the discourse surrounding the situation and the rights of women through the medium of women's magazines, in a moment when women had to reassess their appropriate position in society, politics, and on the labor market. This raises a number of questions: How were women constituted as an identity category in the first place, with their own interests, concerns, and aims? Which ideas about womanhood were constructed and circulated within mass media? And finally, how did they collide and intersect with other identity categories such as worker, activist, or member of an ethnic minority?

Much has been written about the medium of women's magazines, with evaluations of the genre ranging from an oppressive tool of heteropatriarchal society to a medium of empowerment and protest (Forster 4–5). What makes women's magazines notable is that they are explicitly gendered in their target audience, connoting their content as being uniquely relevant for 'women' as a social category.[1] At the same time, the structure of many commercial women's magazines, starting from at least the twentieth century, combines a variety of texts, from literary to practical, from entertaining to informative. What most of these texts share is either an explicit aim or an implicit assumption of giving advice and guidance to their readers, particularly about how to 'be a woman' in various contexts—in relationships, on the labor market, at various stages of the life course, within the family, or among friends (Forster 1–2). This prescriptive tone makes women's magazines a particularly interesting medium to study, in order to trace changing discourses, norms and ideals of womanhood and femininity in a society at a given point in time.

Furthermore, women's magazines are a medium with the potential to form and shape collective identities. In his seminal study on nationalism, Benedict Anderson emphasized the rise of literacy and print capitalism as a key factor for the development of national identity (35–36; 46). Similarly, women's magazines can be argued to have played a role in creating a shared 'identity of womanhood.' Barbara Sato asserts that the

---

1   The target audience does not necessarily correspond to the actual audience. However, the implied audience will usually be obvious to the majority of readers and therefore shape their experience of reading and relating to the text.

rise of mass-produced commercial women's magazines in Japan in the 1920s played an important part in creating a new discourse on womanhood and femininity (78–79). Rising literacy rates and a growing readership, not only among the highest social classes, led to both a standardization in form and a differentiation in themes and topics, as women from different social classes "all forged a place for themselves in their own 'imagined communities'" (Sato 111–112). Sarah Frederick characterizes the increasing popularity of women's magazines as the "emergence of women into public awareness" (3) and argues that the magazines often were the focal point of discussions on 'modernity,' representing both hopes and fears associated with "consumer capitalism, Westernization, and transformation of gender roles" (4). Frederick's analysis pertains to the situation of the interwar period, but, arguably, the same questions resurfaced after the end of World War II when Japanese society was confronted with the democratization policies of the US occupation.

This 'return' of women into public awareness, not just as nationalistic symbols[2] but as a distinct social group, can be understood using Michael Warner's theory of multiple publics and their poetic function of worldmaking (114). Warner argues that the idea of a unified public sphere is ideological and that "it depends on a hierarchy of faculties that allows some activities to count as public or general and others to be merely personal, private, or particular" (117). He contrasts this 'dominant public' with the concept of 'counterpublics' that are not necessarily subversive or radical in nature but a "space for the circulation of discourse" and "for developing oppositional interpretations of its members' identities, interests, and needs" (119). To a certain degree, women's magazines share characteristics of a counterpublic, as they speak to

---

2   Ueno Chizuko argues that wartime mobilization of the population accelerated women's integration into the nation state, but that men and women remained segregated in separate spheres (15; 43–44). Tessa Morris-Suzuki describes this process through a discursive separation of the state as "the domain of the male political actor" and the nation as "natural, nurturing bod[y] . . . often incarnated in feminine form" (110). This allowed for an integration of women into nationalist rhetoric without including them as full citizens.

a group largely excluded from the discourse of the dominant public sphere and are concerned with "mak[ing] their embodiment and status at least partly relevant in a public way" (Warner 58).

Literary texts, in the form of short stories and serialized novels, took up a large part of women's magazines in the postwar period. However, even non-literary articles frequently made use of the narrative form. Authors of articles on a variety of topics related their arguments using anecdotes and stories from their own lives, from history or mythology, while other articles recalled the life stories of not only famous women (ranging from current actresses and writers to historical figures) but also 'common' people. Women's magazines were therefore filled with manifold individual stories of how women in the past and present engaged with questions that most readers were likely to have been confronted with: how to deal with the immediate struggles of everyday life and shortages in food, clothes, and housing (Miki 45–46), but also what kind of future to imagine, regarding women's education and work prospects, marriage and family life, and new-found access to the political sphere. By telling stories of conflict and ways to resolve them, the narratives go beyond merely representing women's lives.[3] Instead, they use narrative tropes and retellings of experiences presumably familiar to the readers, to elicit empathy and identification while rearranging, producing, and reproducing those experiences into their own idealized notions of womanhood and femininity.

A survey of women's magazines in the immediate postwar moment shows that there are three main narrative strategies: firstly, a universalist narrative based on a notion of shared qualities that women were assumed to 'naturally' possess; secondly, a collectivist narrative of solidarity that locates women's identity in a shared experience of oppression; and thirdly, an individualist narrative that also emphasizes shared

---

3   The question of representation and its relation to an ontological reality is its own topic of discussion that considers the position and relation of author, text, reader, and the process of meaning-making that constitutes both our reading of fictive texts and their social surroundings. For a detailed analysis of the debate, see Breger (2017).

experiences but seeks the solution in individual efforts rather than collectivist action.

Universalism and Compassion

The universalist narrative assumes a shared identity of women based
on their 'natural' qualities and character, largely leaving out differences
of class, race, or sexuality. It is closely tied to the trope of women as
being pacifist, kind and caring; and employs motherhood as both symbolic representation and 'rational' explanation for these qualities. An
article titled "The Vow of American and Japanese Grieving Mothers"[4]
that appeared in the popular magazine *Fujin Kurabu* ('Women's Club')
in 1950 contains a conversation between two women from Japan and
the United States, both of whom have lost a son in the Pacific War.
Rather than seeing each other as enemies or blaming each other for
their sons' deaths, they compassionately bond over the shared experience of loss and vow to engage themselves in the peace movement so
that "[no] mother throughout the world [will] experience this painful
grief" (*Nichibei hibo* 61). The article emphasizes the similarity of both
women and their experiences multiple times, particularly in their role
as mothers. It is stated that "feelings of mothers are not different in
America and Japan," and a sub-heading proclaims that "mothers' hearts
are understood throughout the world" (*Nichibei hibo* 64). At the same
time, the political activism in the peace movement that both women
aspire to is clearly demarcated to be one born out of emotion, cast-
ing it in the 'appropriate' field for women's political agency. Yanagiwa
Byakuren, one of the two women, asserts at the end of the conversation that she is "not part of the theoretical (*rironha*) or practical school
(*jissenha*), but a person who is only following her emotions (*tada kanjō
dake de iku kata*)," yet that she still "must raise this prayer of a grieving
mother to the mothers of the world" (*Nichibei hibo* 66).

---

4   All translations from Japanese are my own.

This narrative of a universal experience of woman- and mother-hood, and women being by nature opposed to war, was a common element in peace movements of the 1950s, not only in Japan (Goedde 129). The usage of this trope among women activists was based partly in sincere belief and was partly deployed to gain acceptance for their activism through a gendered discourse (Goedde 133–135). The beginning of postwar peace activism in Japan was split between a conservative and a leftist/communist fraction, with the latter using far more politicized rhetoric than that of the 'pacifist mother' (Yamamoto 135–136). However, in 1950, in the aftermath of the US-occupation's anti-communist 'reverse course' and at the beginning of the Korean War, a more conservative rhetoric dominated, as even less radical peace activism was restricted by the occupation forces (Yamamoto 143–144; Sherif 3).

Collectivism and Solidarity

A second narrative emphasizes collectivism and solidarity, as is dominant in left-wing magazines such as *Hataraku Fujin* ('Working Woman') and *Shin Josei* ('New Woman'). Rather than starting from 'women's nature,' these magazines aimed to mobilize identity on the basis of the shared experience of hardship and oppression specific to women. This happened frequently in the form of transnational comparisons, commenting on the situation and activities of (working) women primarily in China, the Soviet Union, and the United States, and occasionally in European countries. Given the magazine's political outlook, this narrative of shared oppression is frequently and unsurprisingly tied to issues of class and a specific identity of women as workers. In an article in *Hataraku Fujin* from 1949, the author laments that, under capitalism, "the livelihood of workers has been threatened, and lower wages, more frequent layoffs, and even more intolerable humiliations have been forced on women, just because they are women" (Matsuda 16). She goes on to refer to working women as the "most oppressed among oppressed people" (Matsuda 17). The proposition for action in this narrative is a more politicized collectivist attitude that emphasizes solidarity and concrete help and support for fellow (women) workers. Many of these articles simultaneously deconstruct and reinforce essentializing notions of gender. They emphasize the special needs and interests of women but integrate them into a larger narrative of class struggle, as can be seen in a 1947 article by Hani Setsuko, stating that the neglect of women's rights will lead to "never escap[ing] the various forms of hatred and oppression" (Hani 50). Despite the emphasis on women's particular interests, there are also attempts to escape the constraints of rigid ascriptions of femininity or masculinity, calling instead for "a new type of woman" that is neither feminine nor masculine (Hani 51).

This narrative can be placed into the discursive tradition of left-wing internationalism, articulating the fight for rights of specific oppressed groups (based on gender or race) within a framework of class struggle or expressing solidarity for oppressed groups to strengthen support for labor activism. This was a common theme in the "surge of political, creative, and intellectual engagements" (Onishi 107) in early Cold War Japan, which, in addition to left-wing women's groups, also saw movements such as 'Colored Internationalism,' built on notions of Afro-Asian solidarity, and collaboration between *zainichi* Korean[5] activists and Japanese communists in the wake of the Korean War. These solidarity movements constructed race, national identity, and (to a limited degree)[6] gender as identity categories that could be mobilized for activism (Onishi 11–13; Choi 554).

---

5   At the end of the Pacific War, there were approximately 1.45 million Koreans living in Japan as colonial subjects. The majority left Japan after the war, yet around 600.000 remained, and many more returned after initial repatriation (Caprio and Jia 21). After losing their status as 'Japanese subjects,' these *zainichi* ('resident in Japan') Koreans were effectively stateless until 1965, when Japan and South Korea established diplomatic relations, and Japan officially recognized South Korean citizenship (Ryang 7–9).

6   Onishi points out the heteropatriarchal nature of Afro-Asian solidarity movements that often failed to acknowledge women's claims for political agency (Onishi 12). Nevertheless, leftist women's magazines show discursive strategies for establishing gender as a political category that resemble those aimed at integrating race and national identity into solidarity movements.

Individualism and Recognition

The third narrative of individualism is most present in mainstream commercial women's magazines. It appears in countless articles telling the life stories of famous but also lesser-known women. These stories engage with many of the questions surrounding women's new roles in society, such as navigating education and work, marriage and family life, and personal happiness and fulfillment. Many of the stories recognize the struggles and problems women face in society and seemingly question the official narrative of women's liberation through the US-forces and democratization. However, they rarely connect this to political demands but emphasize women's individual abilities and resilience to achieve success and happiness. One example is an article titled "Sugino Yoshiko's Thirty-year Road of Hardships" from a 1950 issue of *Fujin Kurabu*. The article relates the story of Sugino Yoshiko, a fashion designer, and the manifold obstacles she faced in founding and establishing her own fashion school. Throughout the article, she is described as skilled, intelligent, and having an "extremely determined spirit" (*itatte kachiki*) (Yanagawa 83).

In a story about her childhood, she is quoted as stating that "[i]t is not true that a woman cannot become a remarkable person" (Yanagawa 83). In Yoshiko's individual pursuit of a career and personal fulfillment, she challenges conservative Cold War norms of women as housewives that were taking hold in 1950s Japan, but only to a limited degree. When her husband angrily confronts her about working, despite his more than sufficient salary to care for the family, "even the strong-willed Ms. Yoshiko meekly hung her head" (Yanagawa 84). Even though her husband later gives in to her demands and even gives up a promising career opportunity to support Yoshiko's school, the article closes with the statement that the readers should note "the big role that the married love of Mr. and Mrs. Sugino played" (Yanagawa 86) in the school's success, suggesting that a woman's professional career is only possible in the framework of marriage and with the support of a husband.

What these three narratives have in common is the attempt to create a shared identity for women through personal, historical, and transnational narratives. The narratives appeal to empathy, compassion, and feelings of solidarity by relating the hardships, fears, and everyday struggles of women in the changing postwar society. By referencing a shared nature, shared experience of oppression, or individual, yet recognizably 'female' life stories, they represent women as a distinct social group with interests, rights, and demands, while offering models of appropriate behavior and life courses in the wake of changing gender norms. In this way, women arguably emerge as actors and voices in the public sphere. However, it is questionable if women's magazines constitute a '*counter*public,' as defined by Warner, at least regarding his narrower definition of counterpublics as being oppositional and self-aware.[7] The magazines are arguably concerned with creating a 'women's public' while simultaneously attempting to integrate it into the dominant public sphere, whose narratives they frequently reference and incorporate. Rather than constituting a counterpublic, I would argue that the narratives present in Japanese postwar women's magazines are attempts to make women legible as a relevant social category and actors within accepted and normalized discourses of the dominant public sphere.

Bibliography

Anderson, Benedict. *Imagined Communities: Reflections on the Origin and Spread of Nationalism.* Verso, 2006.
Breger, Claudia. "Affects in Configuration: A New Approach to Narrative Worldmaking." *Narrative* vol. 25, no. 2, 2017, pp. 227–251.

---

7   In his analysis of queer counterpublics in particular, Warner emphasizes the experience of stigmatization of the addressed group and the explicit recognition of one's own deviation from the norm within the discourse of the counterpublic (117–118). Despite women's experiences of discrimination, disparagement, and violence, (presumed) heterosexual women seem to be in a different situation, as they are not generally stigmatized on the basis of being women, but rather in response to their resistance to conform to prescribed gender norms.

Caprio, Mark E., and Yu Jia. "Occupations of Korea and Japan and the Origins of the Korean Diaspora in Japan." *Diaspora without Homeland: Being Korean in Japan*, edited by Sonia Ryang and John Lie, University of California Press, 2009, pp. 21–38.

Choi, Deokhyo. "Fighting the Korean War in pacifist Japan: Korean and Japanese leftist solidarity and American Cold War containment." *Critical Asian Studies*, vol. 49, no. 4, 2017, pp. 546–568.

Dower, John W. *Embracing Defeat. Japan in the Wake of World War II*. W. W. Norton, 2000.

Forster, Laurel. *Magazine Movements. Women's Culture, Feminisms and Media Form*. Bloomsbury Academic, 2015.

Frederick, Sarah. *Turning Pages: Reading and Writing Women's Magazines in Interwar Japan*. University of Hawai'i Press, 2006.

Goedde, Petra. *The Politics of Peace. A Global Cold War History*. Oxford UP, 2019.

Koikari, Mire. *Pedagogy of Democracy. Feminism and the Cold War in the U.S. Occupation of Japan*. Temple UP, 2008.

Miki, Hiroko. "Senryō to josei zasshi. 1945 nen kara 1949 nen." *Senryōka josei to zasshi*, edited by Kindai Josei Bunkashi Kenkyūkai, Domesu, 2010, pp. 16–60.

Miller, Jennifer. *Cold War Democracy. The United States and Japan*. Cambridge, Harvard UP, 2019.

Morris-Suzuki, Tessa. *Re-inventing Japan. Time, Space, Nation*. M.E. Sharpe, 1998.

Onishi, Yuichiro. *Transpacific Antiracism: Afro-Asian Solidarity in 20th-Century Black America, Japan, and Okinawa*. New York UP, 2013.

Ryang, Sonia. "Introduction: Between the Nations. Diaspora and Koreans in Japan." *Diaspora without Homeland. Being Korean in Japan*, edited by Sonia Ryang and John Lie, University of California Press, 2009, pp. 1–20.

Sato, Barbara. *The New Japanese Woman. Modernity, Media, and Women in Interwar Japan*. Duke UP, 2003.

Sherif, Ann. *Japan's Cold War. Media, Literature, and the Law*. Columbia UP, 2009.

Ueno, Chizuko. *Nationalism and Gender*. Trans Pacific Press, 2004.

Warner, Michael. *Publics and Counterpublics*. Zone Books, 2005.

Yamamoto, Mari. *Grassroots Pacifism in Post-war Japan. The rebirth of a nation*. Routledge Curzon, 2004.

Primary Sources

"Nichibei hibo no chikai. Kurosubī fujin to Yanagiwara Byakuren joshi no taidan." *Fujin Kurabu*, September 1950, pp. 60–67.

Hani, Setsuko. "Dokuritsu, jiyū, kōfuku." *Hataraku Fujin*, October 1947, pp. 48–51.

Matsuda, Tokiko. "Kokusai fujin dē wo mukaete." *Hataraku Fujin*, March 1949, pp. 16–17.

Yanagawa, Reiko. "Sugino Yoshiko sensei no fūsetsu sanjūnen no michi." *Fujin Kurabu*, September 1950, pp. 82–86.

Notes on the Family Separation Narrative in American Literature: *Uncle Tom's Cabin, Incidents in the Life of a Slave Girl,* and *Lost Children Archive*

Heike Paul

I.

The family, both as a core institution and as a generalized code for intimacy and belonging, has a firm place in the American cultural imaginary. It appears as a guiding metaphor in foundational discourses of the United States and, time and again, serves as a dominant model to channel questions of citizenship, alongside real and imagined kinship. As an "affect saturated" (Berlant) institution, the family (in its various shapes and forms) has also become the site and the vehicle of social and political change. At the same time, throughout US history, the integrity of families has often been threatened and violated by the state and its institutions. In particular, non-white families have been subjected to violent regimes of racialized bondage and displacement. Laura Briggs has documented the history of such separations in her book *Taking Children: A History of American Terror* (2020).

In US literature, issues of family separation are at the center of a sentimental tradition that has long combined aesthetic education and political critique. Based on religious, civil religious, or secular normative underpinnings, the American novel offers affectively powerful plots of family separation that, on the one hand, create moral outrage about acts of violation, while, on the other hand, reflect critically on the supposed sanctity of the (nuclear) family as being the fundamental social unit. In what follows, I discuss the family separation narrative as a literary formula heavily invested in sentimental tropes.[1] As case studies, I draw on the controversial reform novel *Uncle Tom's Cabin* (1852) by the white author Harriet Beecher Stowe, the slave narrative *Incidents in the Life of a Slave Girl* (1861) by Harriet Jacobs, and the more recent text *Lost Children Archive* (2019) by Mexican American writer Valeria Luiselli. All three, I suggest, affectively interpellate their audience and aim at eliciting the preferred feelings (in analogy to Stuart Hall's "preferred readings") of sympathy and fellow empathy; however, while Stowe's text uses the sentimental as an affective narrative strategy to erase difference/alterity, by offering the suffering black subject for identification to a white readership, Jacobs's narrative points to the limits of the resources that the sentimental affords an enslaved mother. Luiselli's novel, in turn, uses representational strategies that preclude easy identification of any kind but engages with the subjectivity of the child in its own right, conveying the affective precariousness of all social ties.

Winfried Fluck has convincingly argued that the Anglo-American sentimental novel (as it was developed in the late 18th and early 19th century) has allowed for specific subject positions to emerge and become the object of empathy: the (fallen) woman, the (abused) child, the (enslaved) black subject. Often, generative sentimental plots aimed at fellow-feeling address the family as the site of both dysfunction and restoration and reveal the conditional and limited autonomy of individual subjects and the importance of social relations. Not surprisingly, narratives of family separation often dramatize social and political injustices and thereby create "affective counterpublics" (Warner) by writ-

---

1   Prior to the emergence of the American novel, Abraham Van Engen identifies the family separation theme in the Puritan archive in texts such as Mary Rowlandson's "captivity narrative" (Van Engen 179). The early American novel takes up and amalgamates earlier literary forms, such as the captivity narrative or the slave narrative. Richard Slotkin and others have pointed out that the slave narrative, in many ways, may be seen as an ideological reconfiguration of the captivity narrative (Slotkin 167).

ing 'along the grain' of normative kinship regimes.[2] The latter often figure prominently, as they serve to de-legitimize practices that run counter to the integrity of families and to the ethos of an individualism that is stripped of any concern with the common good. At the same time, the very notion of what constitutes kinship and 'a family' is also addressed and deepened—in and beyond emotional scenes of family separation and reunion.

II.

Certainly, *Uncle Tom's Cabin* by Harriet Beecher Stowe stands out in the sentimental archive of the 19th century as a novel that is as successful as it is controversial (cf. Paul). The author felt prompted to write it after the passage of the Fugitive Slave Act of 1850. Arguing against the institution of slavery in her text, Stowe has, at the same time, created some of the most powerful and harmful stereotypes about African Americans (cf. Fiedler), for instance, in the figure of Tom. In the beginning, Stowe's novel appeals to its audience by introducing Haley as the most unsympathetic slave trader and exposing his ruthless business scheme in his conversation with Shelby, a financially troubled plantation owner in Kentucky. The child at risk in Stowe's novel is little Harry, the son of Eliza, an enslaved woman in the Shelby household. Readers encounter him in the first chapter of the novel, in a sequence reminiscent of a scene from a minstrel show of the kind that were already spectacularly popular at the time in the North. Harry is playing to Shelby's exhortations, who asks him to perform dances and comical postures (3). Quickly, he is taken away by Eliza, his mother, who experiences discomfort at his exposure in front of the slave trader and at Haley's voyeurism. Following this comic relief for the white men, the maternal melodrama sets in as Eliza learns about the plan to sell Harry to

---

2   The phrase "along the grain" has famously been used by Laura Ann Stoler in her work about the colonial archive. In my usage, it refers to the ambivalence of gendered and racialized representations of kinship in the sentimental text.

Haley, leaving her with no other option but to flee with her son to the North, in order to avoid their separation and to keep him safe. Whereas the title figure of the novel, the slave Tom, is sold to Haley and taken away (he will be brought further to the South and eventually die at the hands of a slave owner), Eliza and Harry become fugitives. Among the most iconic scenes from the book, even though it is only a brief sequence in the narrative, is Eliza stepping on ice floes, carrying her child across the Ohio River to escape her followers and their bloodhounds to the other side, the North. Here, she is helped by several women, among them Mary Bird, a senator's wife, and Rachel Halliday, a Quaker woman. Stowe's heroization of mothers is almost boundless. Throughout the novel, Stowe parades a whole typology of mothers in front of her readers, mostly good, one bad.[3] In her concluding remarks, Stowe's sentimental reasoning takes no excuses from her audience: "But, what can any individual do? Of that, every individual can judge. There is one thing that every individual can do, - they can see to it that *they feel right*" (385, emphasis in the original). It is in the last pages that Stowe seeks to mobilize her (at the time, mostly white and female) readers as an "affective counterpublic" (Warner) by calling on them to empathize and engage in acts of civil protest and disobedience to end slavery.

One stark point of criticism against Stowe's novel concerns its channeling of a black discursivity and its successful fictionalizing of experiences of African Americans as enslaved subjects (Reed).[4] The author disclosed her sources in *A Key to Uncle Tom's Cabin* (1853) to defend her representation of the institution of slavery against her critics. These sources were mostly witness accounts and texts by African American authors, often former slaves themselves. And yet, it was the authority

---

3   Marie St. Clare certainly figures prominently in the novel as the negative prototype of being self-absorbed and lacking empathy.

4   According to sources, Josiah Henson was the model for Stowe's Tom-figure, and he owned this circumstance in his own autobiography. Twentieth-century postmodern African American novelist Ishmael Reed has criticized Stowe and even wrote *Flight to Canada* to mock Stowe for stealing the stories from her enslaved African American contemporaries, turning them into profit.

and the voice of white evangelical womanhood, Stowe's, that, at least for some time, appropriated them and seemed to drown out all of them. In 1861, ten years later, *Incidents in the Life of a Slave Girl*, a slave narrative by Harriet Jacobs, would tell a different story about an enslaved woman successfully escaping from the South with her two children, a story that revealed the ambivalences of motherhood within the institution of slavery. In order to fend off her master's sexual advances, the protagonist of Jacobs's narrative, a mother of a girl and a boy, orchestrates an escape while hiding away in the tiny attic of her grandmother's home on the plantation grounds. Her grandmother is not enslaved, she is free, and she takes care of the children as much as she is allowed to. From the attic, the "loophole of retreat" (173), where Jacobs's narrator hides for years, she can stay somewhat connected with her children in a one-sided way and watch them grow up without ever being seen by them. It is the omnipresent threat of a physical family separation that reveals the perverseness of the system of slavery and which forces Jacobs to take such drastic measures. Only after many years, when the search for her has finally abated, does she make her move, managing to escape with her children to the North. Jacobs's story is obviously sentimental in many respects (cf. Nudelman); yet, she also challenges the normative ideal of the dominant white and middle-class sentimental discourse of her time—often epitomized in a woman's piety and purity—carving out a discursive space for her own experience as an enslaved subject and unwed mother. Consequently, the closure of Jacobs's text resists the pull of respectable domesticity often championed in 19th-century sentimental writing, in favor of sticking to her narrative of emancipation from coercive institutions of all kinds, when she quips: "Reader, my story ends with freedom, not marriage" (302). Hence, Jacobs's *Incidents* speaks back to Stowe's earlier text (and to those of other white female abolitionists, such as Lydia Maria Child, who wrote the introduction). It also anticipates future negotiations of the sentimental in literary texts that continue to produce and reflect on scenes of female suffering, while being less and less invested in resolving them by way of rehabilitating 'the family' according to a normative heteropatriarchal ideal. Considering this, Jacobs' text can be perceived as reprioritizing the so-called cardinal virtues of 19th-century womanhood by placing motherhood ahead of all other normative ideals, such as female purity, piety, and submissiveness.

III.

The legacy of 19th-century abolitionist writing and anti-slavery prose, both autobiography and fiction, can presently be found in contemporary texts that focus not on the Ohio River, as the border between North and South in the US, but further South, on the partially walled US-Mexico border.[5] This space has become the site of a highly militarized border regime and systematic family separations during the Trump presidency, preceded by a decade of deportations throughout the Obama presidencies. A whole range of new texts, again both fictional and non-fictional, addresses the precariousness and subjection of those seeking refuge in the US, among them Diane Winger's *No Direction Home* (2018), Javier Zamora's *Unaccompanied* (2017), Jacob Soboroff's *Separated: Inside an American Tragedy* (2020), as well as the works by Valeria Luiselli: *Tell Me How It Ends* (2017) and *Lost Children Archive*.

Valeria Luiselli's *Lost Children Archive* is a road novel that takes us from New York City to the Southwest borderlands. Four people are in the car, a married couple (man and woman) and two children (boy and girl, 10 and 5 years old). Together they make up a patchwork family, as the woman, and first person-narrator, is the girl's mother, and the man is the boy's father. All of them remain nameless. The adults in the

---

5   Across time, more manifestations of the American family separation narrative come to mind than can be addressed in the space of this essay. In the first half of the 20th century, family separation, as part of schemes of colonization and cultural destruction, has been prominently addressed by Native American writers who chronicle the missionary school education, the disruption of indigenous families, and the coercive practices of adoption. For an overview, see Amelia V. Katansky's *Learning to Write 'Indian': The Boarding School Experience in Native American Literature* (Norman: University of Oklahoma Press, 2005).

car have work projects in the Southwest; the man is researching Native American stories and sounds of the Southwest, in the context of a history of "Indian removal;" the woman is planning a journalistic piece on the deportation of children, another kind of "removal" (Bahadur), and she is also looking for two lost girls about whose whereabouts an acquaintance has asked her to inquire, two of the "lost children."[6] The theme of family separation plays out on two levels in the text. On one level, the border regime and its policy of deportation and family separation are closely observed and documented by the narrator.[7] On another level, it is their own family which is about to fall apart. After a key scene in the novel, in which she and the children witness the deportation of undocumented children being put on a plane (182), the focalization shifts to the boy. He and the girl will eventually run away to look for the two lost girls, the lost children—and in doing so, they will become lost children themselves (237). Contrary to Stowe's and Jacobs's narratives, Luiselli's novel also imagines the subjectivity of the child, the boy. Yet, what the boy identifies as a redemptive, sacrificial move to save the integrity of their own family unit almost ends fatally. The boy and the girl are discovered after days of wandering, but their rescue cannot prevent the break-up of their family, which ultimately also leads to the separation of the siblings.

The novel is experimental in many ways and would hardly be described as a straightforward sentimental text that follows the narrative pattern established in the past. Its postmodern narration and (at times somewhat heavy-handed) intellectual sophistication, in fact, aim at deconstructing any romanticized idea of familial bliss; Susan Sontag is quoted time and again, to provide critical commentary, for in-

---

6   The itinerary in the novel—toward the South and the Southern border of the nation—reverses the direction the immigrants take while walking toward "El Norte."

7   Luiselli began her novel in 2014, and her border tale refers to the deportations during the Obama administration, preceding the harsh measures enforced by his successor.

stance about marriage: "Marriage is based on the principle of inertia" (59). "Inertia" and a road trip do not go well together, and the domestic space has been pretty much dissolved for the time being. Yet, even as the narrative seems to defy sentimental expectations on the reader's side, deconstructing sentimental conventions, for instance, by refusing to give names to its characters, hence leaving not only them in a state of unclaimed vagueness but also their social relations in a generic limbo, its style is nevertheless emotionally charged and evocative in its minimalism. While it is trying to refuse the sentimental, Luiselli's complex novel, with its political critique about conditions at the border, does mobilize emotional responses to the suffering of the children (those children we have come to know, those we see from afar, and others we later learn about). Whether the author is asking her readers like Stowe and others to "feel right," or refuses to do so in any direct way, the sentimental code ultimately elicits empathy and moral outrage and thus affectively mobilizes readers to become politically engaged.

IV.

The family separation narrative appears—in one form or another—in every epoch of American literary history and has a firm place in the transhistorical archive of sentimental writing. Such narratives focus on the violent disruption of the closest social relations, and often, these disruptions are predicated on issues of political and social injustice in a context that has long considered and articulated national politics in the semantics of familial relations and vice versa. The texts briefly discussed here are but three examples. Whereas in the 19th century, writing in the sentimental mode aimed at the institution of slavery, in the 21st century, a similar attempt at abolitionism has turned to other institutions: "Abolish ICE" (ICE: Immigration and Customs Enforcement) was one of the slogans reiterated in the political sphere of activism and protest when Luiselli's book came out, along with #FamiliesBelongTogether. The quests for the well-being of families follow different routes and take different shapes—from Stowe's domestic ideal to Jacobs's ma-

trilineal model, to Luiselli's notion of a much more temporary and fragile social entity, disrupted by both external and internal forces. Family
separation narratives negotiate the conditional autonomy of individuals amidst fundamental/existential social relations; they address responsibilities of care; and they question the terms of 'belonging' in various kinship models. Thus, their criticisms are ambivalent or may even
be explicitly double-voiced: against institutional politics (such as the
separation policies of the state) and hegemonic ideals of the (nuclear)
family, and in favor of *Families We Choose* (as in the programmatic title
of Kath Weston's book). In this two-pronged manner, the family separation narrative has become an ever more complex form of "affective
worldmaking" (Breger) in the sentimental mode.

Bibliography

Bahadur, Gaiutra. "Valeria Luiselli Traces the Youngest Casualties of
the Border Crisis." *The New York Times*, 6 March 2019, https://www.
nytimes.com/2019/03/06/books/review/lost-children-archive-valer
ia-luiselli.html.

Berlant, Lauren. "Poor Eliza." *American Literature*, vol. 70, no. 3, 1998, pp.
635–668.

Berger, Claudia. *Making Worlds: Affect and Collectivity in Contemporary European Cinema*. Columbia UP, 2020.

Briggs, Laura. *Taking Children: A History of American Terror*. University of
California Press, 2020.

Fiedler, Leslie A. *The Inadvertent Epic: From Uncle Tom's Cabin to Roots*. Simon & Schuster, 1979.

Fluck, Winfried. "The Power and Failure of Representation in Harriet
Beecher Stowe's UncleTom'sCabin." *New Literary History*, vol. 23, no.
2, 1992, pp. 319–338.

Henson, Josiah. *The Life of Josiah Henson: Formerly a Slave, Now an Inhabi-
tant of Canada as Narrated by Himself*. 1849. Enhanced Media Publishing, 2017.

Jacobs, Harriet. *Incidents in the Life of a Slave Girl*. Boston, 1861.

Katansky, Amelia V. *Learning to Write 'Indian': The Boarding School Experience in Native American Literature*. University of Oklahoma Press, 2005.

Luiselli, Valeria. *Lost Children Archive*. 4th Estate, 2019.

——. *Tell me how it ends*, 4th Estate, 2017.

Nudelman, Franny. "Harriet Jacobs and the Sentimental Politics of Suffering." *ELH*, vol. 59, no. 4, 1992, pp. 939–964.

Paul, Heike. "Harriet Beecher Stowe, Uncle Tom's Cabin: Or, Life Among the Lowly (1852)." *Handbook of the American Novel of the Nineteenth Century*, edited by Christine Gerhard, de Gruyter, 2018, pp. 281–297.

Reed, Ishmael. *Flight to Canada*. Simon & Schuster, 1976.

Soboroff, Jacob. *Separated: Inside an American Tragedy*. Harper Collins, 2020.

Slotkin, Richard. *Regeneration Through Violence: The Mythology of the American Frontier, 1600–1800*. Wesleyan UP, 1973.

Stoler, Ann Laura. *Along the Archival Grain: Epistemic Anxieties and Colonial Common Sense*. Princeton UP, 2010.

Stowe, Harriet Beecher. *Uncle Tom's Cabin*. 1852. New York: Norton, 1994.

——. *The Key to Uncle Tom's Cabin*. Jewett, 1853.

Van Engen, Abram C. *Sympathetic Puritans: Calvinist Fellow Feeling in Early New England*, Oxford UP, 2015.

Warner, Michael. "Publics and Counterpublics." *Public Culture*, vol. 14, no. 1, 2002, pp. 49–90.

Weston, Kath. *Families We Choose: Lesbians, Gays, Kinship*. Columbia UP, 1997.

Winger, Diane. *No Direction Home*. CreateSpace, 2018.

Zamora, Javier. *Unaccompanied*. Copper Canyon Press, 2017.

Counternarratives and
Community Building

Recognizing Better Selves: A Reparative Reading of Contemporary Bosnian-Herzegovinian Queer Literature

Dijana Simić

> "You have to know: because you were
> there, it was easier for me.
> Moreover, know this: [...] [t]here are
> better and more courageous ones to
> come."
> *Lejla Kalamujić*[1]

In her short prose text "Bella Ciao" (2015),[2] Lejla Kalamujić's autobiographical narrator describes her distant yet still strangely intimate encounters with Bella, a woman in her Sarajevo neighborhood who fascinated her when she was a young girl. Tenderly, she remembers observing Bella from the corner of her eye, finally discovering her name and occupation as a musician by overhearing the grown-ups talk about her. All dressed up in a festive red blouse with ruffles, she even expected Bella to come with the band to her aunt's wedding and thus waited for

---

1 "Jer moraš znati: zato što si ti bila tu meni je bilo lakše. A znaj i ovo: [...] [d]oći
   će bolje i hrabrije od mene" (Kalamujić, *Zovite* 63).

2 The intertextual allusion to the well-known, anti-fascist song "Bella ciao" is evident. It can be understood as the ideological background against which the narrator reflects the marginalization of queer people. She even declares: "They say, the time of struggle will come. I know it will." — "Kažu vrijeme borbe će doći. Znam da hoće" (Kalamujić, *Zovite* 62).

her arrival. Later on, disappointed by Bella's absence, the young narrator deliberately looks for her in the nearby streets and cafes. But only after the war in Bosnia-Herzegovina do the two women meet again. At that time, the narrator is already a teenager, conscious of her feelings and fully aware of what she previously described as the normality of wanting to be close to Bella (Kalamujić, *Zovite* 59).

Not articulating her lesbian identity explicitly, the narrator makes use of "the language of silence" ("jezik tišine"; Kalamujić, *Zovite* 62), familiar to generations of queer people and reflected in Bella's reserved behavior. Retrospectively, she recalls wanting to ask Bella about her life, her experiences with other women, and the historic meeting points of their community. However, at every chance of an encounter, the narrator herself eventually withdraws. Accordingly, she witnesses the same restraint in other—especially elderly—queer people she meets in public: "I want to ask them, where did your loves sprout? Which passages, which hallways, which curtains hid you? I understand the fear in their eyes. And that they act like they do not see me, do not hear me. That they make sure that our bodies don't accidentally touch in passing. I understand. I learned the language of silence."[3] Only after Bella's death does the narrator address her in thought, asking Bella to forgive her for taking so much time to express her gratitude for Bella's mere existence, which made it easier for the young lesbian narrator to understand herself.

---

3   The text "Bella Ciao" is published in Kalamujić's prose collection *Zovite me Esteban* (2015), which was translated into English by Jennifer Zoble as *Call me Esteban* (2021). Nonetheless, the English translations in this essay are mine, D.S. — "Ja bih da ih pitam, gdje su nicale vaše ljubavi? Koji su vas to prolazi, koji haustori, koje zavjese skrivale? Ja razumijem strah u njihovim očima. I to što se prave da me ne vide, da me ne čuju. Što paze da nam se tijela slučajno u prolazu ne dotaknu. Ja razumijem. Naučila sam jezik šutnje." (Kalamujić, *Zovite* 62).

In the chapter "Zlato mamino" (2016, Golden child),[4] Lamija Begagić's narrator Alma describes a similar scene. After suffering an injury, the former table tennis player visits her Bosnian-Herzegovinian hometown, Zenica. Her girlfriend Ivona, with whom she lives in Zagreb, joins her. During their visit, the two women find themselves in a sports center in Doboj to support the young athlete Hana at a table tennis tournament. While waiting for the match to start, they drink coffee on an outdoor terrace surrounded by a handful of other spectators. Carried away by the moment, Alma starts to vividly fantasize about passionately kissing Ivona in front of everybody else. Interestingly, her fantasy is quickly interrupted by Ivona's smile, implying that she understood what was on Alma's mind: "She is smiling at me and winking. She knows everything, she understands everything . . . . Ivona understood that secret language of looks we had to use in places like these. All these years of life on the margins, in the hallways of the lesbian underground, have refined her senses to perfection."[5]

Both Kalamujić's and Begagić's narrators offer insight into queer lives in Bosnia-Herzegovina at the turn of the 20th to the 21st century. In reaction to the marginalization they face, queer people have developed protective strategies of passing that the narrators refer to as "the language of silence" or "the secret language of looks." Begagić's narrator understands these strategies as communicative codes of their own, allowing her and her girlfriend to share a sense of intimacy and belonging in the public sphere. At the same time, as Kalamujić's narrator implies, this silence makes it more difficult for queer people to

---

4   "Zlato mamino" (Golden Child) is a chapter in Begagić's first novel *U zoni* (2016, In the zone), which can also be read as a collection of stories. Interestingly, Kalamujić's *Zovite me Esteban* is a collection of short prose that can be read like a novel. Both authors' short texts function as complete pieces of literature in themselves, but at the same time, they form a greater whole by telling selected aspects of their protagonists' lives.

5   "Smiješi mi se i namiguje. Sve zna, sve je shvatila. . . . Ivona još kako razumije taj tajni jezik pogleda koji moramo voditi na mjestima poput ovog. Sve ove godine života na rubu, u hodnicima lezbejskog podzemlja, istesale su joj čula do savršenstva." (Begagić, *U zoni* 126).

connect and exchange their experiences since they cannot openly approach one another or address their particular concerns publicly. Instead, they are left alone with the unpleasant feeling of uncertainty, wondering whether they interpreted the silent communication of bodily movements and looks correctly. Investigating strategies and structures of queer life writing through the example of autobiography, Brian Loftus describes this phenomenon as "speaking silence."

This oxymoronic syntagma can be construed in two ways: a speaking *silence* encloses so much of the unspoken as well as the unspeakable that it proverbially speaks volumes, while *speaking* silence accentuates the act of articulating the previously unspoken and unspeakable. The selected literary texts address both aspects: the first by acknowledging the phenomenon of "the language of silence," the second by telling their queer protagonists' stories as a means to break the silence. Furthermore, as Kalamujić's lesbian narrator implies, learning about other queer people's lives and recognizing oneself in their life stories can provide the affirmative feelings of reassurance, relief, and reparation: "You have to know: because you were there, it was easier for me." Moving from the literary text to its audience, the narrator's realization serves as an impetus for further reflections about affirmative reception processes. By combining Eve Kosofsky Sedgwick's concept of *reparative reading* with Rita Felski's definition of *recognition* as a particular "use of literature," the present essay aims at understanding what the articulation of queer experiences in contemporary Bosnian-Herzegovinian literature, as a means of challenging the mentioned silence—or rather silencing—might mean for its readers in general and its queer audience in particular.

Understanding Recognition Through Reparative Reading

In her groundbreaking essay, "Paranoid reading and reparative reading, or, You're so paranoid, you probably think this essay is about you"

(1997),[6] Eve Kosofsky Sedgwick describes what Paul Ricœur has termed "the hermeneutics of suspicion" as the dominant approach in literary criticism, which has been so influential that it can be understood as being synonymous with critique itself. Characterized by a sharp-witted reader, a true critic who is ahead of all others, urging to disclose systems of oppression and to deconstruct power relations in texts, Sedgwick calls these methods of interpretation—purposefully exaggerated—*paranoid readings*. Such readings are anticipatory, reflexive, and mimetic; they constitute a strong theory of negative affects; and they place their faith in exposure. In turn, theorizing out of any other stance than the suspicious or paranoid, as Sedgwick states, has been devalued as "naïve, pious, or complaisant" (Sedgwick 126). Without denying the gravity of oppression, Sedgwick replies to this reduction by introducing her idea of *reparative reading* (124–130).

Sedgwick develops her notions of paranoid and reparative reading following psychoanalyst Melanie Klein's distinction between the paranoid-schizoid and the depressive position as a means to describe interpersonal relationships starting in early childhood (object relations theory). While for Klein the paranoid-schizoid position is characterized by alertness to dangerous part-objects in one's surroundings, "the depressive position is an anxiety-mitigating achievement . . . : this is the position from which it is possible in turn to use one's own resources to assemble or 'repair' the murderous part-objects into something like a whole" (128). Accordingly, Sedgwick transfers these observations into the realm of literary studies and interprets the mentioned shift as a "*seeking of pleasure* (through the reparative strategies of the depressive position)" (137), manifested in forms of literary critique that are centered around positive and affirmative affects.

---

6   Wiegman shows that this essay's origins lie in the introduction "Queerer than fiction" of the 1996 special issue of *Studies in the novel*. In a revised form, the essay was included in Sedgwick's 2003 collection *Touching Feeling. Affect, Pedagogy, Performativity* (8–9). Here, Sedgwick's 2003 edition is cited.

Speaking of the "reparative turn" in queer studies,[7] Robyn Wiegman points out Sedgwick's long-lasting influence on queer theorists such as Ann Cvetkovich, Heather Love, and Elizabeth Freeman, who approach their objects of study through "affection, gratitude, solidarity, and love" rather than focusing on "correction, rejection, and anger" (Wiegman 7). Keeping in mind the present essay's interest in reading queer literature in a reparative manner,[8] Sedgwick's often-cited illustrative closing remarks seem to be of particular importance: "What we can best learn from such practices are, perhaps, the many ways selves and communities succeed in extracting sustenance from the objects of a culture—even of a culture whose avowed desire has often been not to sustain them" (Sedgwick 150–151).[9]

While building on Sedgwick's critique of the hermeneutics of suspicion in her book *Uses of Literature* (2008), Rita Felski surprisingly does not mention Sedgwick's notion of reparative reading in her observations. Felski solely determines that it is time to "risk alternate forms of aesthetic engagement" (Felski, *Uses* 4). Referring to John Guillory to strengthen the position of the lay reader, compared to the professional literary critic, Felski describes four possible affective responses to literary texts under the heading of "uses of literature": recognition, enchantment, knowledge, and shock. Formulating a phenomenology of

---

7   Despite her emphasis on reparative reading, Sedgwick gives credit to paranoid reading styles as being crucial constituents of queer theory in the 1980s (126), which concentrated on the investigation of homophobia and heterosexism.

8   Sedgwick addresses queer reading practices explicitly: "Where does this argument leave projects of queer reading, in particular?" (146) In this context, it is important to stress that queer reading and the reading of queer literature are not necessarily the same. In the present essay, the latter is in focus.

9   Ann Cvetkovich describes holding on to the positive aspects, in spite of the negative ones, as "a profoundly queer sensibility": "Thus, if I began with depression and close on utopia, I have not necessarily shifted topics or even affective registers—the point would be to offer a vision of hope and possibility that doesn't foreclose despair and exhaustion. It's a profoundly queer sensibility and one that I hope can enable us to tackle the work that needs to be done and to create the pleasure that will sustain us." (467).

reading, Felski looks at how certain phenomena disclose themselves to the reader through literature (Felski, *Uses* 12–17).

Asking what it means to recognize oneself in a book, without falling into the trap of self-centered narcissism and risking a trivialized interpretation of art, Felski explains that the literal meaning of recognition is "knowing something again," adding: "we make sense of what is unfamiliar by fitting it into an existing scheme, linking it to what we already know" (25).[10] Therefore, recognition is a cognitive process through which readers get to know themselves better after reading a book. Literature plays a particularly important role in recognizing oneself when other forms of acknowledgment are missing in one's direct surroundings. In this case, individual as well as collective readings offer long-desired solace, relief, and escape from the fear of invisibility, or —to evoke Kalamujić's and Begagić's texts—from silence, "confirming that I am not entirely alone, that there are others who think or feel like me" (33). Here, the meaning of recognition in literary studies coincides with its definition in political theory. For political theorists, recognition does not mean knowledge but acknowledgment. Thus, the claim for recognition is a claim for acceptance, dignity, and inclusion in the public sphere. While recognition in reading is oriented toward the self, in political theory, it is oriented toward others. As shown, this distinction is not a dichotomy since "the question of knowledge is deeply entangled in practices of acknowledgment" (30).[11]

In her subsequent book, *The Limits of Critique* (2015), Felski explicitly builds her argument on Sedgwick's theory of reparative reading, understanding it to be one mode of what she defines as *postcritical reading*: an engagement with the literary text that goes beyond the dominant hermeneutics of suspicion without being uncritical, by combining critical reading practices with the consideration of positive affects. Conse-

---

10   Felski criticizes the assumption that recognition requires direct resemblance by emphasizing the aesthetic qualities of literature with its multifaceted, metaphorical, and self-reflexive dimensions (Felski, *Uses* 44).

11   Felski investigates the correlation between feminist literature and feminism as a social movement in her book *Beyond Feminist Aesthetics* (1989).

quently, instead of interrogating what a text undermines, the postcritical reader, according to Felski, is eager to comprehend: "What does this text create, build, make possible?" (*Limits* 182).

Reading Queer Literature in Bosnia-Herzegovina

In 2017, the activist Nera Mešinović, one of the organizers of Bosnia-Herzegovina's first pride march in 2019, wrote an article for the online platform *lgbti.ba* about a public reading of Lamija Begagić's novel *U zoni* (2016, In the zone) at one of the biweekly LGBTI-meetings at the NGO *Sarajevski otvoreni centar* (Sarajevo Open Center, SOC). The article is accompanied by a photo probably taken by one of the organizers or spectators, maybe even by Mešinović herself. Judging by the quality and angle, the photo was likely taken with a phone, while sitting on the floor next to the author. It shows a group of young people sitting closely around the author. The venue seems to be the office of SOC, transformed into a space for public events (like this literary reading). In the background, there are bookshelves and working desks. A carefully arranged rainbow flag is hanging on one of the walls, next to organizational information printed on white paper. Furthermore, there is a cardboard figure in the background, maybe a leftover from a previous art installation or activist intervention, or maybe just a piece of decoration. Begagić smiles softly while some of the participants take notes and others pictures. All of them seem to be listening carefully. The depicted atmosphere feels intimate since people sit close to each other, leaning towards one another, smiling or looking curiously at the author and moderator, Sandra Zlotrg. Some of the participants even stand in the hallway, which implies that all seats in the room were already taken, indicating that the event was well visited.

Mešinović begins her report by acknowledging the day of the reading—March 27th, 2017—as being a milestone in the history of queer art in Bosnia-Herzegovina, due to the presentation of Begagić's text as the first Bosnian-Herzegovinian lesbian novel. She emphasizes the novel's significance by describing the participants' lively involvement in the discussion and their collective bodily resonance to the text, in moments of synchronized laughter. Situated within SOC's biweekly LGBTI-gatherings, it is not surprising that the literary reading attracted members of Sarajevo's queer community, opening up a discussion about queer literature in Bosnia-Herzegovina. When asked about her novel's classification as queer literature, Begagić answered that the novel's queerness is not indicated by the fact that the protagonist is lesbian but rather the lesbian protagonist's confrontation with the society in which she lives. In this respect, Mešinović reflects upon the novel's political implications: "The context within which the novel is written, and within which the story takes place, is Bosnian-Herzegovinian society, for which it is indispensable to write about lesbian heroes to conquer the public space as well as space for political activity."[12] Read in a Felskian manner, Mešinović's closing remarks touch on aspects of recognition through literary readings, as she interprets the participants' engagement in the discussion as a confirmation of the power of art to create space for questioning one's own identity.

Speaking about queer literature in an interview with Bojan Krivokapić for the Belgrad-based leftist magazine *Mašina* (Machine), Kalamujić emphasizes the emergence of queer literary festivals and writing contests in the post-Yugoslav space after 2000: *Šarolika pera* (Colorful quills) in Sarajevo, *Write Queer* in Podgorica, *Srečanje LGBT literature ex-YU* (Meeting of LGBT literature of Former Yugoslavia) in Ljubljana, etc. While she observes an expansion of queer literature as a specific genre through these platforms, she also notices its integration in the literary mainstream, manifested in the inclusion of queer authors and their texts in anthologies, as nominees for literary prizes, etc. She explains this recent development through a focus on the intersections of queer, feminist, and class-related issues as the most challenging questions in contemporary post-Yugoslav societies. She argues that, by putting

---

12   "Kontekst u kojem djelo nastaje, i u kojem se odvija, je kontekst bh. društva za koje je neophodno pisati o junakinjama lezbejkama da bi se osvajao javni prostor i prostor političkog djelovanja." (Mešinović).

the minoritarian discourse about queer lives into perspective through broader questions of class, it becomes evident that the deprivation of rights forms the basis for a common struggle of a disenfranchised majority. Taking into account that neoliberal capitalism promotes the idea that society has reached a supposedly post-ideological state, characterized by individualization, she states that imagining alternatives to the current conditions becomes almost impossible. Therefore, Kalamujić highlights the political potential of literature to stimulate readers to imagine—we might quote one of Begagić's titles here—"better selves," since literature offers an enormous spectrum of different contents and forms. Without reducing literature's value to plain utilitarianism, Kalamujić sees literature's main function as returning to readers what they feel they have lost: "To offer us a broader picture of the world and ourselves."[13]

In an interview with Tamara Zablocki for the aforementioned website *lgbti.ba*, Begagić similarly acknowledges literature—besides having multifaceted aesthetic value—as a platform for political activism, stressing the importance of hopeful narratives that nurture optimistic visions of the societies they depict. Her newest collection, *Bolji mi* (2020, Better Selves), bears witness to the author's reparative stance: never fully neglecting the disheartening aspects of queer lives, Begagić's text, "Siguran Space" (Safe Space), talks about the openly lesbian teacher Nina who supports her student, Sanjin, in his coming-out process. His family's accepting reaction, which comes as a surprise for the student, is contrasted with Nina's experiences of being open about her sexuality in her public life as a teacher, while being unable to talk about it to her father in the private realm. Similar to Bella and Lejla from Kalamujić's story, Nina and Sanjin belong to two different generations. In this regard, the transgenerational change in their own perception, as well as their surroundings' perception of queer sexuality and identity, implies a hope for the better—or as Kalamujić's narrator puts it: "[t]here are better and more courageous ones to come."

---

13   "Da nam ponudi neku širu sliku svijeta i nas samih." (Kalamujić in Krivokapić, "Queer").

Queer Literature, Community Building, and the Public Sphere

Understood in a reparative sense, the selected examples of contemporary Bosnian-Herzegovinian queer literature reveal two dimensions of recognition offered by literary texts. First, recognition in a classical Felskian sense comprises the potential for readers to recognize themselves in literature. It's this dimension of recognition to which the two authors Kalamujić and Begagić, as well as the activist Mešinović, refer in their readerly practices, when they stress the reader's ability to question their own identity through literary examples that offer them a more nuanced picture of themselves. Second, the representation of moments of recognition in literary texts constitutes another dimension of recognition. In this sense, Begagić's character Ivona recognizes her girlfriend's desire to kiss her in public as her own, in a similar way as Kalamujić's narrator Lejla apprehends her own sexuality and identity by recognizing Bella as a lesbian: "Then, I could already understand you. Understand myself."[14] Based on the previous considerations, the first dimension can be defined as recognition *through* the text, whereas the second can be identified as (a representation of) recognition *within* the text. As marked by the intimate public reading at SOC, both dimensions are intertwined in multifaceted ways. This opens up further questions about the correlations between queer literature, community building, and the public sphere.

In this regard, Mešinović's claim to "conquer the public space," when referring to the publication of Begagić's lesbian novel, as well as the lesbian protagonist within this novel, can be understood more profoundly through Felski's, Fraser's, and Warner's queer/feminist revisions of Jürgen Habermas's public sphere theory. Namely, these scholars emphasize narratives in general and literary narratives in particular as being constituent elements of *counterpublics*, which Nancy Fraser defines as "discursive arenas where members of subordinated social groups invent and circulate counterdiscourses, which in turn permit them to formulate oppositional interpretations of their identities, interests, and

---

14   "Tad sam već mogla razumjeti tebe. Razumjeti sebe." (Kalamujić, *Zovite* 60).

needs" (Fraser 67). Highlighting the correlations between feminist literature and feminism as a social movement, Felski (*Beyond* 167) demonstrates the manifestation of a specifically feminist counterpublic. When considering literature's role in the constitution of counterpublics, Felski's work can be effectively connected to Michael Warner's understanding of publics—and, therefore, also counterpublics—as text-based "mediated publics" (61), "mediated by print, theater, diffuse networks of talk, commerce, and the like" (56–57). To summarize, I return to Felski's previously mentioned question: "What does this text create, build, make possible?" (*Limits* 182). By breaking the aforementioned silence and narrating queer people's marginalized life stories from queer perspectives, a queer counterpublic is being established *in* as well as *through* the selected literary examples of contemporary Bosnian-Herzegovinian literature. Similar to Kalamujić's narrator, who believes that there are more courageous ones to come after her, I believe that these future authors' life writings will inspire further and more detailed investigations that connect literary studies, affect studies, and public sphere theory.

Bibliography

Begagić, Lamija. *U zoni*. Fabrika knjiga, 2016.

Begagić, Lamija. *Bolji mi*. Fabrika knjiga, 2020.

Cvetkovich, Ann. "Public Feelings." *South Atlantic Quarterly*, vol. 106, no. 3, 2007, pp. 459–468.

Felski, Rita. *Beyond Feminist Aesthetics: Feminist Literature and Social Change*. Harvard UP, 1989.

Felski, Rita. *Uses of Literature*. Blackwell Pub, 2008.

Felski, Rita. *The Limits of Critique*. U of Chicago P, 2015.

Fraser, Nancy. "Rethinking the Public Sphere: A Contribution to the Critique of Actually Existing Democracy." *Social Text*, vol. 25/26, 1990, pp. 56–80.

Kalamujić, Lejla. *Zovite me Esteban*. Dobra knjiga, 2015.

Krivokapić, Bojan. "Lejla Kalamujić: Queer, feminizam i klasno pitanje su najjači uzbunjivači društvene stvarnosti." *Mašina*,

2000, https://www.masina.rs/lejla-kalamujic-queer-feminizam-i-klasno-pitanje-su-najjaci-uzbunjivaci-drustvene-stvarnosti/.

Loftus, Brian. "Speaking Silence: The Strategies and Structures of Queer Autobiography." *College Literature*, vol. 24, no. 1, 1997, pp. 22–44.

Mešinović, Nera. "Roman 'U zoni': Lezbejska ljubavna priča sa zeničkih ulica, oživljena u sjećanju." *lgbti.ba*, 2017, https://lgbti.ba/roman-u-zoni-lezbejska-ljubavna-prica-sa-zenickih-ulica-ozivljena-u-sjeca nju/.

Sedgwick, Eve Kosofsky. "Paranoid reading and reparative reading, or, You're so paranoid, you probably think this essay is about you." *Touching Feeling. Affect, Pedagogy, Performativity*, edited by Eve Kosofsky Sedgwick, Duke UP, 2003, pp. 123–151.

Warner, Michael. "Public and Private." *Publics and Counterpublics*, edited by Michael Warner, Zone Books, 2005, pp. 21–64.

Wiegman, Robyn. "The Times We're In: Queer Feminist Criticism and the Reparative 'Turn.'" *Feminist Theory*, vol. 15, no. 1, 2014, pp. 4–25.

Zablocki, Tamara. "Lamija Begagić, spisateljica: Svi naši aktivizmi mogu se voditi i u književnosti." *lgbti.ba*, 2020, https://lgbti.ba/lam ija-begagic-spisateljica-svi-nasi-aktivizmi-mogu-se-voditi-i-u-knj izevnosti/.

Where are the Lesbian Rom-Coms? Building Reparative Narratives Through Fan Creativity

Iveta Jansová

The announcement of the release date for the holiday romantic comedy *Happiest Season* in December 2020 caused a colorful response from audiences, fans, and even media professionals. *Happiest Season* is a holiday-themed lesbian romantic comedy starring Kristen Stewart and Mackenzie Davis. While there have been similar movies recently (e.g., *Lez Bomb*, 2018 or *Season of Love*, 2019), they did not have such a popular ensemble (including Aubrey Plaza, Dan Levy, and Clea DuVall in the director's chair).[1] Although the holidays always bring with them many new seasonal romantic comedies, LGBTQIA+ stories remain mainly in the background of these or are entirely absent in holiday-related content.

Even if non-heteronormative storylines (such as the lesbian storylines mentioned above[2]) concern the media, no matter the season, people yearn for light, positive, feel-good stories, especially during cheerful holiday times, as well as in sad and scary times, as the COVID-19 pandemic undoubtedly is. However, if our identity does not conform to the mainstream in some aspects (e.g., race or sexuality), we might not find "our" content as much as we would like. This is precisely the reason why we need to question the whereabouts of lesbian romantic

---

1   Not including the movie *Carol* (2015) or *Ammonite* (2020) is intentional here, as they are period pieces and fall into different genre categories (with strong dramatic features commonly portrayed by "more popular" ensembles).

2   Due to the essay's narrow scope, I primarily pay attention to the exemplary category of lesbian narratives.

comedies or "light-hearted" narratives (and of course those depicting other identities), even more so, since existing productions reveal very repetitive tendencies in the portrayal of lesbian and queer stories.

A brief survey of the existing "lesbian movie library"[3] shows that a variety of movies does exist, a substantial number of which are period pieces (e.g., *Tipping the Velvet*, 2002; *Fingersmith*, 2005 or *The Favorite*, 2018 and *The Portrait of a Lady on Fire*, 2019), tragic narratives (e.g., *Gia*, 1998; *Aimée & Jaguar*, 1999; *Lost and Delirious*, 2001; *Freeheld*, 2015), or coming out (and coming of age) stories. And, there are also some comedies (e.g., *But I'm a Cheerleader*, 1999; *Saving Face*, 2004; *Imagine Me & You*, 2005). However, these pale in comparison to the overwhelming number of raw, heartbreaking, and very often unrelatable narratives.[4] Such tiring repetitiveness of similar (if not identical) depictions can become frustrating, thus prompting some audience members to retaliate. Thereby, the current state of lesbian identity media portrayals can become a source of critique, inspiration, and even reparation for its audiences, particularly fans. By creating their own narratives and endeavors that have been more or less derived from mainstream production (movies, TV series, comics, music, etc.), fans offer new venues for portraying marginalized identities that differ from the recurring storylines to which we have become so accustomed. Such derivative creative work can be seen as a manifestation of the theoretical concepts of polysemic decoding of media texts, as conceptualized by Stuart Hall (1973), and reparative reading strategies introduced by Eve Kosofsky Sedgwick (2020), both suggesting the existence of a countless number of possible

---

3   Such a term is obvious hyperbole. However, there are numerous movies and TV series that are considered to be a sort of "lesbian canon." Movies and series originating between the 1980s to the early 2000s (e.g., *Desert Hearts*, 1985; *Heavenly Creatures*, 1994; *The L Word*, 2004; *I can't think straight*, 2008, etc.) served as one of the first possibilities for many lesbian and queer women internationally to identify with media characters and are thus considered to be a "canon."

4   We often see one-dimensional characters, poor character development, ridiculous narrative changes unrelated to the previous storyline, etc.

readings (i.e., interpretation), stemming from individual (here mostly marginalized) experiences of audiences.[5]

Media fans have played an essential role in discussions about the meanings of media content and in how far the needs of particular marginalized communities were met (or more often not met) in media representation for decades. This essay takes these "conversations" between audiences and producers into closer consideration, while introducing an original perspective on media communication. This particular point of view, which reflects the highly interactive and creative contribution from the audience itself, sheds light on their perception and reworking of the (state of) contemporary lesbian storylines in media.

(Transformative) Creativity of Fans

By the term *media fans*, I mean those audiences interested mainly in TV series and movies, excluding sport, music, or other kinds of fans. In the field of fan studies, media fans are understood as being somewhat different from "ordinary audiences,"[6] mostly in their practices related to engaging with media content. The previous studies often imagined them to be active, loyal, and creative individuals following particular media texts and having an interactive relationship with them (cf. Jenkins; Hills; Busse and Hellekson; etc.).[7] Not only are such fans fond of

---

5   Both terms suggest that audiences can interpret (not only media) content differently and highlight the crucial role of individual identity in those varying interpretations.

6   Of course, the notion of ordinary audiences is problematic in the current "digitalized time." Here, it serves only as an illustrative term, labeling those who do not consider themselves to be fans and who exhibit a more "passive" approach to media consumption/reception.

7   The perception of fans as being exclusively (inter)active is somewhat simplistic. The question of fan identity (mainly related to fan practices) and its proclivities have been discussed in the field of fan studies from its beginning in the 1990s (Jenkins; Hills; Gray et al.). Fans can be very interactive, but they can also stay

certain content, but they can also get creative about it and produce their own texts (e.g., songs, stories, costumes, videos, etc.) in reaction to the original. Such responses vary from pieces celebrating particular content (but also performers, authors, etc.) to a relatively sophisticated critique, both of them in various forms. However, the principle stays the same—there is an original text (e.g., movie/TV series, etc.), and it serves as a starting point for the follow-up creative work of fans.[8] Whatever the motivation,[9] fans borrow their favorite characters or universe to build new stories and worlds within the borders indicated in the original.[10] Fan creativity is, therefore, somewhat apocryphal.

As I have already pointed out, it would be incorrect to think that all fans are creative, active, activist, loyal, and connected (to each other and the original subject/object). However, I will use this premise to explain *transformative creativity* similarities. As previously stated, different kinds of fan creativity stem from the personal relationship towards the particular media text. In general, the central dialectic of such invention is quickly drawn with the help of the terms *affirmative* and *transformative fans/creativity* or fandom—i.e., a group of fans with the same/similar interests (Jenkins et al.). Some fans feel the need to simply reproduce

---

away from common fan practices and be more consumerist. It is hard to imagine some typical fan identity, as it is a deeply individual notion (cf. Jansová).

8   In the context of this text, José Esteban Muñoz's concept of *disidentification* comes to mind. Fans searching for representation (i.e., their marginalized identity) in the media and not finding it can decide to create their own stories in which they negotiate their individuality among the mainstream production that often erases them. With the help of disidentification, queer fans can rework and alter dominant cultural codes in ways that help them "write themselves" into the stories they are so often absent from.

9   Fan creativity is motivated by various reasons—love for the object/subject, critique of the content, coming back to a favorite (yet) finished story, revisiting stories or characters, righting the wrong of media representation, etc. (cf. Jenkins).

10   Circulation of creative work of fans is based on the so-called gift economy, sharing with others without payment but with an expectation of some participation (sharing, liking commenting, etc., cf. Jansová 103–106; Gray et al.).

something/someone in their original work as a sign of their appreciation (e.g., draw a picture of the leading characters). Others return to a story/character they miss (e.g., in case their favorite show ended) or have different motivations that nevertheless resonate (in the final creative product) with the intentions and meanings postulated in the original content. This colorful palate of work can be described as affirmative. However, fan creativity can also stem from different motivations, making room for transformative interpretations.

Just as some content is unreservedly popular among fandoms and fans, other works (or parts of popular works) can have problematic aspects that serve as an impulse for various creative works—starting with simple tweets and discussions, ending with sophisticated videos, stories, costumes and many other manifestations of fan creativity. Activist efforts and campaigns, or even educational efforts, aimed at the favorite content (movie/TV series) can also be considered to be manifestations of this phenomenon. All of the original work, activism, and educational efforts are a form of reaction. Once again, we can encounter countless motivations for such (inherently active) relations towards media content. Most common (in the context of the representation of marginalized identities) are shallow and unrelatable representations (i.e., diversity check[11]), recurring tragic narratives (e.g., *Bury Your Gays* trope, BYG[12]), repetitive storylines, *queerbaiting*,[13] and many others. All of them spark transformative reactions that (in one way or another) try to repair the perceived damage caused by

---

11   Characters are present only to fulfill some invisible "diversity quota."

12   The so-called *Bury Your Gays* trope is a term that fans (and later academics) began to use to describe repeated deaths of non-heteronormative characters on screen (movies or TV series).

13   Queerbaiting is a strategy for attracting as diverse an audience as possible by suggesting a potential romantic relationship between same-sex characters without a plan to realize such a pairing. By hinting at this possibility, it can attract people interested in non-heteronormative pairings, but it will also maintain the interest of conservative audience members because there is no obvious proof of non-heteronormative relations (Jansová 121–125).

media content.[14] The following section shows some examples of how this reparation can be realized.

Fans and Reparative Narratives: A Case of Femslash Fandoms

I started this essay with the example of a lesbian holiday comedy and its meaning within contemporary lesbian narratives. I will stay with the notion of lesbian representation and discuss so-called *femslash* fan's interpretations. The term *femslash* describes a variety of (inherently transformative) creative works by fans that center around lesbian interpretations. It is considered a particular genre of fan creativity defined by the character's romantic pairing.[15] Such interpretations usually rework the original media text (e.g., TV series) and reimagine or reinterpret some of its characters as lesbian, even though they were not presented as such in the original. One example is the popular teen TV series *Glee*, where two of the leading female characters (Rachel Berry and Quinn Fabray) were first introduced as enemies and later became tentative friends. Some fans interpreted their interactions and storylines as an indication of a blossoming romance and created stories that reflected their readings (e.g., written stories, videos, drawings, etc.). The most common motivation in this context is the low number of existing "lesbian representations" in the media and the state of such representation.[16]

---

14   As can be observed in recent years, some reactions or relations towards the original that negate its dominant meanings can cross a symbolic line and become even antagonistic, in so much that terms such as toxic fandom or anti-fans exist to designate similar relations and practices (cf. Garcia Hernandez; Pinkowitz).

15   Other categories are *slash* (gay interpretation of male characters' relationship), *het* (heterosexual interpretation of relationship), or *gen* (general and non-romantic description of relationships).

16   It needs to be pointed out that the number of non-heteronormative characters' representation increases every year. The most rapid changes can be seen since 2016 (cf. GLAAD). Consequently, femslash interpretations also "re-consider" already non-heterosexual storylines, resulting in the creation of *canonical femslash*, as I coined it (Jansová 92).

However, it is impossible to list all the potential motivations that can fuel any kind of "fanish" creativity.

Notwithstanding the rich quantity of different texts, videos, costumes, drawings, pictures, and many others around the world, I can only focus closely on a small number of examples here. As there are countless artworks that would be very hard to choose from and explain in detail, I mainly use examples of fan activism fighting for reparation in the original text. Yet, it cannot be ignored that such activism is very closely connected to all fan stories and interpretations that tirelessly try to repair and reclaim media representations.

One of the most hurtful media tropes regarding the representation of lesbian characters and storylines is the aforementioned *Bury Your Gays* trope. BYG is a term describing sudden, unexpected, and usually unnecessary deaths of LGBTQIA+ characters that are often mindlessly used to move the story along (for the primarily heterosexual characters), as can be seen in a variety of media content (e.g., *Last Tango in Halifax*, 2012; *Pretty Little Liars*, 2010; *The 100*, 2014; and many others). In 2016 and 2017, there were several protests against such (frequent) depictions that resulted in many "fanish" activist campaigns. Not only were there thousands of Twitter discussions and challenges towards media creators,[17] but several educational and supportive campaigns were established as well. Two examples are the internet site *LGBT fans deserve better*[18] and the fan convention *ClexaCon*. These efforts reflect the state of LGBTQIA + characters in the media. At the same time, *ClexaCon* "brings together thousands of diverse LGBTQ+ fans and content creators worldwide to celebrate positive representation for LGBTQ+ women, trans and non-binary communities in the media" (ClexaCon).

The launch of this initiative was primarily prompted by the death of the character Lexa in the TV series *The 100*, which is why it carries

---

17   One of the most discussed examples happened in the context of *The 100* TV series. The show's producer, Jason Rothenberg, apologized to fans for using the BYG trope, but only after he lost more than 14 000 of his previous followers on Twitter (cf. McNutt, 2017; Bourdaa, 2018)

18   Available from: https://lgbtfansdeservebetter.com/.

the name of the central lesbian pairing Clexa (i.e., a portmanteau of their names: Clarke and Lexa). The death of Lexa also brought about many cases of reparative narratives aimed at soothing the hurt caused by the TV series' original storyline. Looking through the main archives of written fan fiction (e.g., FanFiction.net or Archiveofourown.org), we see hundreds of stories that imagine carefree and—staying on the topic of "rom-coms"—humorous adventures of the favorite pair. Thanks to such re-workings, we get to see Lexa either as a standoffish millionaire, falling in love with the struggling student Clarke, or as a star soccer player, hilariously (and romantically) colliding with the new team doctor, Clarke. Simply put, the favorite duo is offered an entirely different ending but also a life on the pages of those fan stories.

These practices of writing extensive and complex stories, thereby initiating protest and activist campaigns, are not just indicative of the scale of emotional, financial, and other investments in media content. They also reflect another specific characteristic of fan-driven identity practice—namely, community building. With *femslash* interpretation, we see quite a unique phenomenon. Particular fans around the world create a symbolic community that we can label as lesbian fandom. Even if such a notion can feel simplifying, we genuinely see international connections with a common goal—to produce and share quality "lesbian media content" that resonates with different experiences and identity manifestations.

Conclusion

Consequently, certain types of fan creativity (here *femslash*) can be considered reparative and even as counter-narratives. Fans substitute undesirable content/stories with their own creative works, repairing the (perceived) damage caused by media representation of different identities (mainly marginalized) or reworking them in new (counter) narratives, showing that the topic can be dealt with in entirely different ways. Thanks to those "grassroots narratives," we can see/read/perceive a variety of experiences, desires, and possibilities of narrating marginalized stories that remain underrepresented in mainstream media, even while mainstream movies such as *Happiest Season* or *The Prom* (both released in December 2020), featuring canonical lesbian relationships, are becoming more common.

However, as audiences seem to take things into their own hands, we no longer have to count on mainstream representation. In the maze of different TikTokers, YouTubers, and other creators who share their personal (but of course fictional, e.g., web-series) stories through the social network sites, we become privy to countless narratives resonating with varying types of identities. But does this really mean that we do not need (and want) to be included in mainstream popular culture (i.e., movies and TV series) anymore? Additionally, the (slowly) rising number of LGBTQIA+ representation in mainstream and alternative media brings to mind the question of (homo)normativity. Might we be witnessing a further spread of post-gay representation (cf. Monaghan), normalizing "nice and shiny" non-heteronormative identities and silencing their counter/reparative/activist voices?

Bibliography

Bourdaa, M. (2018). "May we meet again": Social bonds, activities, and identities in the #Clexa fandom. In *A Companion to Media Fandom and Fan Studies*.

ClexaCon. Our Vision. 2020, [online] available from: https://clexacon.com/about/vision/.

Garcia Hernandez, Y. "Latina fans agitate respectability: Rethinking antifans and antifandom." *Transformative Works and Cultures*, vol. 29, 2019.

GLAAD. "Where We Are on Tv." *Media Institute*, 2019.

Gray, Jonathan, et al., editors. *Fandom: Identities and Communities in a Mediated World*, 2nd ed., New York UP, 2017.

Hall, Stuart. *Encoding and Decoding in Television Discourse*, 1973.

Hills, Mathew. *Fan Cultures*. Routledge, 2002.

Jansová, Iveta. *(Bez)mocní mediální fanoušci: Televizní serial jako zdroj bojů o význam mezi fanoušky a producenty.* Univerzita Palackého v Olomouci, 2020.

Jenkins, Henry. *Textual Poachers: Television Fans and Participatory Culture.* Routledge,1992.

——, et al. "Spreadable media: Creating value and meaning in a networked culture." *Cinema Journal*, vol. 53, no. 3, 2013, pp. 152–77.

McNutt, Myles. "'The 100' and the social contract of social TV." *Transformative Works and Cultures*, vol. 26, 2018.

Monaghan, Whitney. "Post-Gay Television: LGBTQ Representation and the Negotiation of 'Normal' in MTV's Faking It." *Media, Culture & Society*, vol. 43, no. 3, April 2021, pp. 428–443.

Muñoz, José Esteban. "Introduction: Performing Disidentifications." *Disidentification: Queers of Color and the Performance of Politics*, U of Minnesota P, 1999.

Pinkowitz, Jacqueline M. "Praxis rejection of excess in Twilight Antifandom." *Transformative Works and Cultures*, vol. 7, 2011.

Sedgwick, Eve Kosofsky. "Paranoid Reading and Reparative Reading, or, You're So Paranoid, You Probably Think This Essay Is About You." *Touching Feeling: Affect, Pedagogy, Performativity*, edited by Michèle Aina Barale et al., Duke UP, 2003, pp. 123–152.

Shaping Gender and Kinship Relationships in Recent Croatian Satirical Fiction

Renate Hansen-Kokoruš

Why should we research the treatment of gender and kinship relationships in satirical literature? What is the connection between these topics and satirical writing, and how might such a study be helpful for a discussion of narrative counterpublics? As a preliminary hypothesis: satire allows for critical distancing from societal and private grievances and thus provides an opportunity for forming alternative relationships. This paper discusses foundational positions concerning the characteristics of satire and connects these to the presentation of gender and kinship. Of central importance is the question of how satire involves readers and shapes their imagination and reactions. I will explore these questions by discussing the novels and screenplays of Ante Tomić, a popular satirical author from Split.

In theoretical discussions of its general attributes, satire as a mode[1] is typically understood to be a form of literature, mass media, or an aesthetic creation.[2] It is not confined to written expression (Quintero 9), and it (generally) attacks societal or individual grievances based on positive moral values. In combination with an attitude of aggression, the

---

1   See Breunig 66 and Mahler 23ff., Hempfer, Brummack 355, Schwind 19ff., Zymner 21, 23. Satirical genres will not be discussed here, nor the many types of satire.

2   See Condren 661, Arntzen 1989, 15, Breunig 69, Brummack 356, Schwind 19ff., Wölfl 304.

social function of morality, aesthetic techniques, humor,[3] and the influence of the reader's elicited mental and emotional reactions[4] are essential. Although the latter belongs to the most frequently addressed open questions of literature, satire undoubtedly aims to awaken the reader's desire for reform, or even seeks to resolve the issues it raises. Nevertheless, satire cannot automatically be identified with subversiveness (Condren 662). It depends on whether partial changes in the character's or the text's subject's—the abstract author's—worldview are intended, indicating either a progressive or conservative viewpoint. This is abundantly clear in the highly popular genre of comedy, which uses humor in different ways to critique grievances, shortcomings, or behaviors. Common stereotypes concerning marginalized groups sometimes serve as a source of laughter, and even the imagined exclusion of the other may become central to comedy.

Consequently, humor is conceptualized in vastly different ways.[5] Theorists such as Georg Lukács claim that satire has no subversive potential if it makes use of humor, criticizing tendencies towards "conciliation" and "liberal forbearance" regarding the criticized circumstances. Thus, Lukács argues that satire helps to minimize aggression towards problems within society and reconciles the reader with injustices in the world. Other theorists who share this position connect satire to the systematic societal sublimation of critical thought and see its fundamental function in the aesthetic control of aggression instead of social activity (cf. Weiß 11). However, humor and irony are of crucial importance to satirical texts and serve not only to reduce emotional tensions but also to reinforce subtle meanings. Ironic utterances, in which a given wording significantly differs or even contrasts with the intended meaning, bind the reader to the text's subject—because both are connected

---

3   See Frye 109, Arntzen 1989, 15–16, Condren 661.
4   See Brummack 358, Breunig 72, Condren 662, Zymner 21.
5   The problem of humor, linked to the manifold functions of laughter, is a complex topic and will not be addressed in detail in this paper (see, for instance, Bergson, Bachtin, Huizinga, Voss).

by the secret knowledge that what is said should be interpreted anti-
thetically and not be taken at face value. However, the effects of humor
differ, based on its expression: accusing humor, mocking, and excluding
of entire groups have the same effect, but only in cases where readers
do not belong to or empathize with the lampooned. This kind of humor acts according to fixed categories and confirms existing opinions.
Conversely, sympathetic humor (in Lukács' understanding, reduced to
being bourgeois and soft) is able to transcend fixed borders, improve
reader's positions, and change their attitudes.

Through fictional presentation and ambiguity, satire creates a specific relationship with the reader. Irony and a strategy of dissimula-
tion (Wölfel 297), or dissimilated lying, belong to its basic methods. As
Mahler states in his definition, satire is "a speech act that consciously
transgresses rules of conversation, disingenuous, but at the same time
is transparent to the listener in its insincerity, . . . a secondary use of
given patterns of speech."[6] Thus, the reader recognizes the narrated
world from a distance as being artistically alienated[7] but, at the same
time, familiar. Narrator and intended reader are confidentially linked,
since the implied author seeks to make the reader the narrator's or the
protagonist's mental and emotional companion. This is only possible if
the narrator does not discriminate or offend the reader, which would
hinder their partial identification with the character or the narrator.[8]

---

6   "eine Konversationsmaximen absichtlich verletzende, unaufrichtige, aber in
      ihrer Unaufrichtigkeit vom Hörer gleichwohl durchschaute Sprechhandlung,...
      eine sekundäre Indienstnahme vorgegebener Sprachmuster." (Mahler 43; see
      also Wölfel 297, Zymner 22).

7   Alienation can be the result of different techniques, but the attack of the
      general—not the detailed—phenomenon is one of its common characteristics
      (Arntzen 572; Wölfel 85). Thus, even if details are more central, they are never
      the primary target, as satire always requires the reader's abstraction from the
      concrete to the more general attribute below the surface of phenomena.

8   Such texts fit into the genre of pamphlet or pasquil, understood as being mo-
      tivated by private resentment (Arntzen 181) and with the aim of destroying a
      rival (Zymner 22).

Thus, attacks against human or societal deficiencies have to be tempered by positive attitudes that offer a chance for identification and reform to the reader. Depictions of stereotypes can be problematic, as they are often used for negative generalizations.

When considering the depiction of gender and kinship relations in recent Croatian literature, we come across the genres of detective fiction and romance in popular literature, commemorative/autobiographical, and "biographical" literature. These texts deal with personal and/or historical taboos of Yugoslavia or Croatia (i.e., the treatment of political "enemies" in labor camps or the German minority), social and cultural references, topics of everyday life, or insights into intimacy. Whereas many novels focusing on political "taboos" show very problematic kinship relations between children and their parents,[9] as a consequence of prevailing silence about historical circumstances, Ante Tomić's novels present recent everyday topics in a popular and satirical manner.[10]

In Tomić's novels and films based on such themes, we are often confronted with—unsurprisingly—traditional gender and kinship relations of heterosexual couples. His male characters are well-to-do officers, lawyers, businessmen, politicians, farmers, teachers, or even priests. His female protagonists appear in the roles of housewives, nurses, hairdressers, servants, workers, or students who have low incomes or are dependent on their husbands.[11] The way gender and kinship relations are portrayed is mostly stereotypical and exaggerated but still familiar to the reader's experience: typical examples include not only the search for love and an ideal partner but also extramarital affairs of well-situated husbands. However, what makes Tomić's work

---

9   See Hansen-Kokoruš, 2013.

10   His popularity finds its expression in the number of editions and films based on his novels. The films are among the most popular Croatian film productions in the past 15 years and have received many awards at international film festivals.

11   There are also well-to-do women, but they are often presented in a negative and stereotypical light: for example, a young pop-star without musical ability, relying on financial and cultural support from her rich boyfriend's family.

significant is a creeping, step-by-step shift from the dominant perspective of men to the marginalized outlook of women, which ultimately becomes central in many texts. Indeed, even in strong patriarchal kinship structures (manifested in the 'clan'), matrimonial tendencies emerge (for example in *Čudo u Poskokovoj Dragi*, 2009, The Miracle in Viper's Glen).

Lidija, the protagonist in *Ljubav, struja, voda & telefon* (2005, Love, Electricity, Water & Telephone), rushes headlong into a marriage dominated by her husband and his family, especially his "mama." The young woman breaks out of her life as a housewife,[12] in favor of a life without material security, working as a hairdresser while self-determinedly flouting convention and embracing new ways of life. What makes this character convincing and refreshing is Lidija's anti-authoritarian behavior and colloquial speech, which gives her authenticity,[13] her fearlessness and the categorical rejection of subordination to patriarchal men, and her attempt to control her own life. Her history shows different kinds of women's oppression (from her own family traditions, her husband, his family, and her married lover). Thus, the story generally discusses its manifold manifestations: emotional blackmail (by her friend Branka and her importunate boyfriend), the fear of articulating sexual desires (embodied by the conservative women in Lidija's beauty salon), and the fear of transgressing conventional boundaries (Lidija demands payment for sex). The implied author makes use of an incredibly canny technique. The character of Lidija presents herself to the readers as a radical but authentic and true woman whose desires are understandable: she wants love with all her heart and searches for a partner without any kind of subjugation or loss of self.[14] Her life experience

---

12   Her husband's traditional understanding of women's duties is shown in one particular detail: his symbolic gift for their wedding anniversary is an apron with the motto "My wife is the best cook."

13   She uses the idiom of Split, which is quite vulgar and provocative.

14   Thus, the author plays with stereotypical expectations and shows the socially conditioned nature of gender images. The comic effects are caused by the switch in gender roles, as Lidija's behavior is more typical of men.

leads more and more to her refusing to lie. Speech is her weapon—as is common in male self-portrayals—and she evokes sympathy due to her lack of pretension; however, when talking to her small son, she communicates in an entirely different manner, showing her to be a more conventional loving mother.

Tomić avoids the creation of a completely stereotypical character by also depicting her desires and doubts as to whether she is on the right path. However, one technique is of special importance for the persuasiveness of this figure: she narrates from a first-person perspective. As we know, this influences the reception of a character—readers regard the information as trustworthy and accurate, even the narrator's gender. Surprisingly, Tomić uses a cross-gendered, first-person narrative: the male author chooses a female narrator, a technique which Ingrid Noll also used effectively in her crime novel *Stich für Stich* (1997, Stitch by Stitch), a story in which the protagonist narrates "her" story of tragic alienation from her partner, in the first-person, until the reader ultimately realizes that the artistic handiwork is linked not—as expected—to a woman but a man. Humor is the other decisive method that plays a key role in the positive reception of this and other characters: Lidija articulates what others are afraid to even imagine in a liberating way. Transgressing taboos of permitted communication is what makes the readers laugh. Thus, reading the novel may lead women, in particular, to identify with this sharp-tongued, quick-witted character that offers a sense of emancipated partnership. In other novels about patriarchal kinship structures, Tomić presents women as the strong gender who solve the problems, underlining their mental power, empathy, and intelligence.

The 2016 film *Ustav Republike Hrvatske* (The Constitution) and its screenplay (2017) also show how satire challenges mainstream opinions regarding gender and other relations; they combine stereotypes of straight and same-sex relationships with ideological statements of politics and religion,[15] while demonstrating their absurdity. Two popular

---

15   The conservative social and ideological commitment of the Catholic church is one of Tomić's most passionate issues and the topic of two more of his novels.

positions stand in contrast: Vjeko Kralj (the surname means "king"), a strong conservative, nationalistic bourgeois teacher with strong prejudices against other nationalities and classes, is living a double-life as a closeted gay man who—in contrast to his own prejudiced worldview—is also portrayed as a character full of sympathy, mourning his partner who committed suicide and searching for compassion.[16] He is connected to Croatian history through his fascist father, a caricature of the Ustaša movement, whose ability to act is—figuratively and literally—amputated and who despises same-sex relationships. On the opposing side, there is the working class in the basement, the policeman Ante and his dominant wife Maja Samardžić, a nurse. The teacher, representing the upper class, shows no respect for them, due to their Serbian origins and lower level of education. Maja, however, transcends her antipathy for her snobbish neighbor, through a clever deal: she cares for Kralj's father. Kralj, in turn, tutors Ante in the Croatian constitution for an exam required for his promotion. As a result, their original disrespect for one another gradually decreases. They gain a mutual understanding and even grow sympathetic to one another's attitudes. The idealized conclusion of the film is hyperbolic but nevertheless offers an optimistic core, presenting two rigid and opposing worldviews and lifestyles, initially unwilling to change their positions. Both sides come into contact—not by choice but by necessity or even fate—and learn to accept the other's alterity. Maja's and Ante's

---

Što je muškarac bez brkova? (2005, What Is a Man Without a Moustache?) focuses on the abolishment of clerical celibacy, embedded within a romantic love story initiated by a woman. In Veličanstveni Poskokovi (2014, The Great Vipers), the Catholic church is depicted as one of the greatest political and financial powers of Croatia, involved for centuries in the corrupt misrule of the country.

16   The film mixes these categories more than the scenario, creating comic effect: the actor who plays the Croatian teacher is a well-known Serbian actor (Nebojša Glogovac, who died only a few months after the film's completion). The fact that an anti-Serbian, Croatian nationalist is also gay and played by a Serbian actor challenges the idea of clearly defined and stereotypical identity categories. The film poster visualizes mixed representations of gender by showing the Croatian/Serbian man in make-up and in female clothes.

stereotypically portrayed relationship grows deeper, as they attempt to adopt a child. The optimistic view does not simply lead to the coexistence of two parallel worlds. Rather, their connections liberate them almost automatically from their ethnic, religious, sexual, and other prejudices.

In conclusion, satire can challenge traditional gender and kinship relations by emphasizing empathy through its critical characters. Stereotypes serve as a hyperbole for deficiencies and are supplemented by other attitudes[17] to underline that they are changeable. In this way, the narrative avoids rejection by readers by circumventing any impression of personal attack. Irony undermines negative attitudes and evokes a kind of "corrective laughter" (Condren 661), which gives the reader the feeling of being included in the worldview of the text's subject. Thus, the reader is invited to identify with a critical position and to self-reflect, which is more acceptable when it is accompanied by humor than by strong attacks. The strength of satire is not the presentation of alternative ways of life but rather the activation of critical thinking. However, the transformation of actual political and private relations is left to the readers.

Bibliography

Arntzen, Helmut. "The Satiric Mode of Feeling." *SATVRA: Ein Kompendium moderner Studien zur Satire*, edited by Bernhard Fabian. Georg Olms, 1975, pp. 178–193.

Breinig, Helmbrecht. *Satire und Roman: Studien zur Theorie des Genrekonflikts und zur satirischen Erzählliteratur der USA von Brackenridge bis Vonnegut.* Narr, 1984.

Brummack, Jürgen. "Satire." *Reallexikon der deutschen Literaturwissenschaft*, vol. 3, de Gruyter, 2003, pp. 355–360.

---

17   The individual, reality-based, more positive attitudes are accompanied by empathy for the respective characters' motives. This enables readers' identification with those characters, even when they offer new worldviews and images.

Condren, Conal. "Satire." *Encyclopedia of Humor Studies*, edited by Salvatore Attardo, Sage, 2014, pp. 661–663.

Frye, Northrop. "The Nature of Satire." *SATVRA: Ein Kompendium moderner Studien zur Satire*, edited by Bernhard Fabian, Georg Olms, 1975, pp. 108–122.

Hansen-Kokoruš, Renate. "Formen adoleszenter Infantilität und ihre Funktion." *Kind und Jugendlicher in der Literatur und im Film Bosniens, Kroatiens und Serbiens*, edited by Renate Hansen-Kokoruš and Elena Popovska, Dr. Kovač, 2013, pp. 17–36.

Lukács, Georg. "Zur Frage der Satire." *SATVRA: Ein Kompendium moderner Studien zur Satire* edited by Bernhard Fabian, Georg Olms, 1975, pp. 425–449.

Mahler, Andreas. *Moderne Satireforschung und elisabethanische Verssatire: Texttheorie, Epistemologie, Gattungspoetik*. Fink, 1992.

Quintero, Ruben. „Introduction: Understanding Satire." *A Companion to Satire*, edited by Ruben Quintero, Blackwell, 2007, pp. 1–11.

Schwind, Klaus. *Satire in funktionalen Texten: Theoretische Überlegungen zu einer semiotisch orientierten Textanalyse*. Narr, 1988.

Tomić, Ante. *Što je muškarac bez brkova*. Hena Com, 2005.

——. *Ljubav, struja, voda & telefon*. Ljevak, 2012 [2005].

——. *Čudo u Poskokovoj Dragi*. Ljevak, 2009.

——, and Rajko Grlić. *Ustav Republike Hrvatske*. Hena Com, 2017.

Voss, Christiane. "Lachen." *Komik: Ein interdisziplinäres Handbuch*, edited by Uwe Wirth, Metzler, 2017, pp. 47–51.

Weiß, Wolfgang. *Die englische Satire*. Wiss. Buchgesellschaft, 1982.

Wölfel, Kurt. "Epische und satirische Welt. Zur Technik des satirischen Erzählens." *SATVRA. Ein Kompendium moderner Studien zur Satire*, edited by Bernhard Fabian, Georg Olms 1975, 294–307.

Zymner, Rüdiger. "Satire." *Komik: Ein interdisziplinäres Handbuch*, edited by Uwe Wirth, Metzler, 2017, pp. 21–25.

Filmography

The Constitution: A Love Story About Hate, directed by Rajko Grlić., performed by Nebojša Glogovac, Ksenija Marinković and Dejan Aćimović, In Film, Interfilm, Revolution, and Sever & Sever, 2016.

Quick Media Feminisms and the Affective Worldmaking of Hashtag Activism

Silvia Schultermandl

Introduction

"Another week, another hashtag, and with it, a question about what is actually being accomplished," quips *The New York Times*' David Carr in 2012, in his polemical piece "Hashtag Activism, and its Limits." Carr expresses concern about an over-simplified conflation between the ubiquity of hashtags and radical social change and is skeptical about social media's agentive possibilities: "If you 'like' something, does that mean you care about it?" The dichotomy Carr insinuates, that liking and becoming active cannot be reconciled, seems oddly out of step with the political events of his own historical moment—after all, 2011 was the year of the Arab Spring—and in the age of *#BlackLivesMatter* and *#MeToo*, the valence of social media for political activism is evident: hashtag activism is part of a larger repertoire of the political, and hashtags have been appropriated by political movements on all ends of the ideological spectrum. That hashtag activism leads to real consequences can be seen in a number of prominent cases, such as the conviction of Harvey Weinstein for rape and sexual assault in March 2020 and the mobilization of the white nationalists who stormed the US Capital in January 2021. Furthermore, as Caroline Dadas contends, the "attention" hashtag activism generates often includes acts of retaliation, both in the form of online hate speech and violations of privacy through doxing or deep fakes.

Nevertheless, I want to take Carr's question about caring to heart and raise issues about the circulation of affects via hashtags. I do so by looking at what I call *quick media feminisms,* the mobilization of feminist thought and activism via quick media, "an umbrella term for the cheap, easily accessible, and omnipresent tools of communication which allow us to connect to each other spontaneously and effortlessly and which include both messaging platforms such as text and Skype and social media outlets such as Facebook and Twitter" (Friedman and Schultermandl 4). Quick media feminisms include many instances of hashtag activism,[1] *#MeToo* perhaps being the most widely known, but they also include feminist practices in closed-forum digital spaces on Facebook and feminist art projects that adopt quick media affordances and properties. They are simultaneously cultural artifacts and dynamic archives of contemporary social practices which record the development of feminist thought in the face of various political and social challenges of the present historical moment. While, of course, not all quick media usage is feminist, quick media can facilitate counter-hegemonic spaces and serve as a platform for feminist activism, allowing users to express resistance, create visibility, and organize and mobilize communities.[2] However, the same online spaces archive the hate speech posted to challenge and misappropriate these projects' original intent, truth claims, visibility, and traction. Therefore, quick media feminist projects

---

1   The term "hashtag activism" was first introduced by Eric Augenbraun in his 2011 piece on the Occupy Wallstreet movement in *The Guardian*.

2   Scholars in media studies have worked extensively on the effects of quick media usage and their impact on communicative practices, social relationships, consumerism, political activism, and the generation of critical masses in a variety of contexts; see Jennifer Earl for a comprehensive overview of this scholarship. With critical insights into phenomena ranging from the democratization of information to data mining, scholarship in this field pushes existing definitions of identity, individuality, and community to new limits, especially in scholarship on online cultures and intersectionality (Dobson; Friedman 2013, 2018; Haraway; Nakamura; Nakamura/Chow-White; Noble; Noble/Tynes; Poletti/Rak; Young; Zimmerman).

also record conversations between different politically oriented counterpublics and the vicious reactionary responses they incur. These responses are rife with contributions from members of groups such as
the Incels, the various red pill crowds, and *#meninism* folks that defend
white cis-hetero male privilege against gender equity, political correctness, and other aspects of social reform they perceive as directly dis-
criminating against them. The affect which circulates in these spheres
is perhaps best described by what Kate Manne calls "himpathy," the re-
direction of sympathy away from the cis and trans women who experience harassment or abuse and towards the men whom these women
allegedly expose, in an attempt to end their careers and destroy their
idealized heteronormative families (197).[3] Hence, from a cultural studies perspective, quick media feminisms are interesting for the kinds of
issues they raise, contributing to a diversification of ideas about body,
identity, gender, nationhood, and other categories of difference; equally
interesting is the way in which they circulate affects through the dis-
putes they incite and record and the affective worldmaking to which
they contribute.

In my essay, I want to attend to these two levels of quick media
feminism by analyzing the following feminist interventions: *@DearCat-
callers*, a project on Instagram where a young woman posts selfies
with the men who catcalled her; *#YouOkSis*, a consciousness-raising
and community-building platform on Twitter; and *#CatcallsofGraz*,
a collective project which creates murals out of the sexist messages
that anonymous users share with the organizers of the platform.
All three quick media feminist projects seek to counter the incurred
objectification through catcallers by taking back agency, by putting the
catcallers and their speech acts on public display, and by facilitating a
space of resistance. They therefore emphasize quick media's potential
to constitute feminist counterpublics, in which a different form of
being in the world becomes possible.

---

3   Such was the criticism launched at Dr. Christine Blasey Ford when she testified
     against Supreme Court Nominee Brett Kavanaugh, in 2018, on account of sexual
     misconduct during their college years.

All three projects document instances of verbal abuse, but it is important to emphasize that verbal harassment is never just verbal: it is also somatic and visceral, linked to feelings of vulnerability and—in some cases—the anticipation of physical harm. As my discussion of various examples will show, these posts evoke the circumstantial contexts in which harassment occurs: Why does this context register as particularly endangering? Are there other people close by who register as trustworthy, and can you trust your sense of judgment in such times of crisis? How much has your sense of agency been manipulated by narratives of shame, blame, and more of the same?

Online Counterpublics and the Affective Economies of Quick Media

The role of quick media in creating and sustaining counterpublics has been amply discussed in a variety of disciplines, ranging from work on the discursive interpellation of counterpublics through social media to theorizations of quick media via affect studies. The latter foreground the affective worldmaking, which comes into existence through quick media's particular formal properties and affordances, including their interactive, rhizomatic, relational, and phatic nature. In life writing studies, quick media have challenged prevalent understandings of authorship, text, and the self in relation to the dynamics of the web.[4] In addition, theorizations of publics and counterpublics have begun to account for quick media's media-specific particularities. In *Affective Publics: Sentiment, Technology, and Politics*, Zizi Papacharissi contends that a hashtag allows "for crowds to be rendered into publics; networked publics that want to tell their story collaboratively and on their own terms. These networked publics come together and/or disband around bonds of sentiment" and convene "across networks that are discursively rendered out of mediated interactions" (308). Similarly, danah boyd

---

4   See also Zizi Paracharissi's work on the "networked self;" and Laurie McNeill's "There is no I in Network" on questions of the posthuman self.

proposes that networked publics include "(1) the space constructed through networked technologies and (2) the imagined collective that emerges as a result of the intersection of people, technology, and practice" (39). Such definitions of online counterpublics adapt Michael Warner's emphasis on counterpublics' "circulation of discourse" (80) to account for the ubiquity and dynamic circulation of posts, likes, and tweets.

The accessible, collaborative, and potentially connective narratives circulating via quick media cohere around a shared sense of identity, experience, and belonging. Susanna Paasonen, for instance, argues that "where the affective, somatic, and the cognitive stick and cohere, resonance helps in understanding online connections and disconnections, proximities and distances between human and non-human bodies" (51). Similarly, Papacharissi contends that "[a]ffective attachments to media cannot produce communities, but they may produce 'feelings of community'" (*Affective Publics* 9). Which kinds of affective responses they elicit can, of course, not be readily determined but depend on the ideological configurations emerging from the emotional, somatic, or visceral responses between readers, characters, and authors (see Breger in this book). The well-known example of *#nastywoman*, which emerged in October 2016 during the US presidential election, is a case in point. On the one hand, users employed this hashtag in acts of resistance against misogyny, thereby giving the idiom of the "nasty woman" a positively connoted subversive meaning; on the other hand, users adopted this hashtag as a misogynistic moniker designed to extend the insult initially launched at Hillary Clinton to other women in politics. As examples from January 2019 show, posts with feminist icons and pro-life criticism of liberal politics become conjoined via the same hashtag and thus document the contentious debates centering on feminist politics. Figures like the nasty woman are "sticky, or saturated with affect, as sites of personal and social tension" (Ahmed, *The Cultural Politics of Emotions* 11) and can therefore mobilize different ideological groups. What initially started as a feminist quick media intervention against misogyny and broke with the slurs' interpellatory violence, by giving it a subversive resignification, eventually became a shorthand for the organization of diametrically opposed political projects.[5]

This adherence of different affective economies to the same sticky figure also exemplifies the micro-aggressions which are part of the misogynistic repertoire of everyday sexism. Quick media's specific affordances make such micro-aggressions easily available for circulation. And while, according to Lisa Nakamura, they "tend to be discounted as not real, but rather part of the virtual world" (337), they are indicative of the same large-scale systemic misogyny against which quick media feminist projects protest. As the by now robust scholarship on #MeToo illustrates, quick media feminisms track the relationship between feminist activism and the subsequent anti-feminist backlash.[6]

The three quick media feminist interventions I discuss below exemplify the discursive and material strategies through which quick media feminist projects connect and mobilize counterpublics. They traffic in what Sara Ahmed terms "affective economies," around which feelings of belonging cohere ("Affective Economies" 117). By citing specific cases of harassment and depicting viable strategies of resistance, quick media feminist projects call attention to the ubiquity of public harassment. At the same time, their online representation and dissemination debunk prevalent assumptions that verbal harassment is merely a grey area issue of public safety. In addition to materializing moments of witness and testimony, they index the social climate surrounding misogyny by capturing the various politically significant responses to individual posts and tweets.

---

5   See Judith Butler's *Excitable Speech: A Politics of the Performative* for details on practices of subversive resignification.

6   See, for instance, Boyle, Karen's *#MeToo, Weinstein, and Feminism* (2019), and Bianca Fileborn and Rachel Loney-Howes' edited collection *#MeToo and the Politics of Social Change* (2019).

@*DearCatcallers* and the Refusal to Laugh Along

@*DearCatcallers* is an Instapage created by award-winning Dutch artist Noa Jansma to showcase the extent, range, and frequency of catcalling she received, all of which ostensibly were intended to be compliments on her body, sexuality, and femininity.[7] For an entire month (September 2017), she posed with her catcallers and posted the resulting selfies. Of the 28 posts she put up, 22 are selfies with catcallers, accompanied with verbatim quotes of the things they said to her. The project's subtitle, "It's not a compliment," puts the various quips she received into perspective by emphasizing the malign intent of any form of public harassment. Through Twitter, #*DearCatcallers* went viral instantly: over 300,000 people actively followed it, some posts have over 6400 likes and almost 800 comments. The project, which officially concluded at the end of September 2017, continues to live on in many forms, including Jansma's solo photo exhibition, interviews, and Ted talk appearances.

While Jansma's project was designed to turn the public sphere into a safer space for women, the virtual world in which it circulated is anything but safe. This may be attributed to the confrontational nature of her project, but it is also related to networked interactivity, which, according to Laurie McNeill and John David Zuern, relies on a "many-to-many structure, with a range of participants being private in public" (xi). This notion of being private in public via online technologies also reminds us that online narratives are inherently relational and that a person never composes their life narratives themselves or on their own terms. If we think of online life writing not solely as a narrativization of one's own life, via quick media outlets, but also as the inadvertent tracking, tagging, and monitoring that occurs in the background, we have to concede that multiple versions of our online life narratives coexist at the same time, always in specific and particular ideological contexts.

In the case of Jansma's project, what mobilized these publics are the various affective economies bearing on the issue of sexism, women's

---

7   Among other accolades, Jansma won the Dutch Gouden Kalf Beste Interactive in 2018.

rights, and gender-based discrimination at large. Jansma's project received three distinct kinds of responses: posts that partake in her outrage against everyday sexism; hate speech in the form of slut-shaming and rape threats directed at her; and posts that mildly side with the catcallers who they feel are being unjustly exposed on her Instapage. All three groups coalesce around shared feelings of empowerment, threat, or pity, respectively, and the affective economies of these communities and their spontaneous formation via quick media. Certainly, Jansma's project was borne out of feminist consciousness raising, but, as mentioned above, among the responses its interactive nature invites, it also features sexist hate speech. Such posts cite "political correctness," "cancel culture," and "genderism" as oppressive interventions of a liberal elite, and the authors of such posts use Jansma's platform to protest what they think of as misandry. To groups that oppose equal rights initiatives, Jansma's project epitomizes the "norms of the dominant culture" (Warner 80), which they feel unfairly censors them. What was intended as a contribution to dismantling sexism now circulates in forums where the verbal abuse Jansma first encountered is not only repeated but frequently grossly upstaged, probably precisely because she went public with the private. In her 2018 project *DearHaters*, Jansma published the conversations *@DearCatcallers* inspired and notes that 75% of them are hate speech.

With these comments as a backdrop, Jansma's selfies with the catcallers center on her assertion of agency in the face of objectification. Together with her control over the image (and perhaps, by extension, the situation), her unamused but determined gaze serves as a commentary to the laughter and ridicule most of the men in her selfies express. Jansma's refusal to partake in their humor and laugh it off exemplifies a feminist resistance strategy that Sara Ahmed terms the "feminist killjoy" (*Living a Feminist Life* 10), a deliberate rupture with the banter that racist or sexist comments often solicit. Through her non-compliance, Jansma's feminist killjoy-pose underscores the gravity of misogyny and other forms of systemic violence against women.

#YouOKSis and Care as Feminist Praxis

My second example, the hashtag *#YouOkSis* revolves around solidarity and care. It resonates deeply with black feminist work on love as political activism and positions mutual care as a feminist intervention against harassment in the public sphere. The hashtag *#YouOkSis* indexes the collective action of passersby who witness and intercept harassment directed at black cis and trans women on the street and in the cybersphere. Most posts report specific incidents of verbal abuse or stalking and mention the action taken against them. A cursory read through the posts indicates an even distribution between posts referring to actions taken by the person who reports the event and posts witnessing others' expressions of solidarity and civil courage against what Moya Bailey terms "misogynoir."[8] The hashtag was launched by Philadelphia-based feminist activist, artist, educator, and social worker Feminista Jones,[9] in an attempt to highlight the particular vulnerabilities of black cis and trans women. A well-known contributor to Black Twitter, with *#YouOkSis*, Jones facilitates a platform where people can share strategies to de-escalate situations potentially leading to physical harm and to memorialize the lives of women who have been murdered in city streets.

The predominant affective repertoire circulating via *#YouOkSis* draws largely on the notion of care. Besides its Black vernacular characteristics (Johnson 69), the familial question "You ok, Sis?" evokes a sense of intimacy in the tradition of feminist sisterhood and, at the same time, serves as a code of mutual recognition available to persons sensitized to the shapes and forms of harassment. With this emphasis on caring for one another, Jones's project connects to a well-established tradition of Black feminist activism which defines love and care as political practices. Black feminist scholars and activists, including Audre Lorde, June Jordan, and bell hooks, devised intersectional strategies

---

8   See her forthcoming book *Misogynoir Transformed* or her Tumblr post from 2014, in which she introduced the concept to call attention to Black women's particular experiences of misogyny.

9   This is her professional name; her actual name is Michelle Taylor.

of resistance against systemic racism and sexism based on a shared sense of caring for one's self and one's community. Perhaps most prominent within this tradition of Black feminist theory is Patricia Hill Collins's assertion that "[l]oving Black people ... in a society that is so dependent on hating Blackness constitutes a highly rebellious act" (250). The forms of resistance practices via *#YouOkSis* extend these heuristics into the realm of quick media, but the nascent feeling of a shared sense of suffering and a communal resilience activate a long history, thus honoring a feminist tradition dating back to the radical politics expressed in the Combahee River Collective Statement of the mid-1980s.[10]

The historical dimension of this heuristics is significant for *#YouOk-Sis* because it includes an orientation towards a less hostile future. It bespeaks a desire not only for safety in the here and now but for a prospective outlook that public spaces may become less hostile terrain for cis and trans women. A closer look at the related hashtags, with which contributors to Jones's political project interface, underscores its affinity with other prominent examples of Black Twitter, including *#BlackLives-Matter*. Taken together, the convergence of these hashtags materializes in what Paige Johnson terms a "technocultural assemblage" (62), whose affective worldmaking can perhaps best be understood through Gilles Deleuze and Félix Guattari's understanding of assemblage as "a becoming" rather than "a being." The hashtag *#YouOkSis* registers these dimensions of love precisely because of its affinity with *#BlackLivesMatter*, whose germinal phase started with Alicia Garza's famous declaration of love: "Black people. I love you. I love us. Our lives matter."

---

10   For a succinct discussion of the valence of love in second-wave Black feminism and its anti-essentialist potential, see Jennifer Nash's essay, "Practicing Love."

@CatcallsofGraz and the Material Dimensions of #MeToo Life Writing

My third example employs various forms of remediation to involve random audiences in the memorialization of harassment. @CatcallsofGraz is part of a global project which documents catcalling through chalk graffiti drawn in or outside the public places where it occurred: in front of restaurants, in parks, outside cafes, on campuses. These are some of the locations where the project organizers of @CatcallsofGraz have rendered the fleeting experience of harassment temporarily visible. The various subchapters in different cities in Europe, Asia, and North America indicate a similar practice: the project invites victims of street harassment to DM (direct message) their stories via Instagram, and the organizers of the project "chalk back" by memorializing the event on site, displaying the specific verbal insults in conjunction with their own Instagram name and further referencing #StoppBelästigung (stop harassment). In addition, the project invites people in Graz to meet regularly for a communal chalk back event, where the grievances over sexism and public harassment, together with consciousness-raising initiatives against femicides, surface outside city hall and equally prominent places. Due to the robust media coverage by local news outlets, the initiative has gained considerable notoriety in Graz. The fact that @CatcallsofGraz is becoming a readily accessible and popular site to report harassment is exemplified by a case in late January 2021, where several women reported sexual harassment at a city-run COVID testing facility.

The chalk graffiti, which publicly memorialize harassment, employ a particular affective aesthetic strategy. The DIY aesthetic of chalk graffiti in bright colors combines the children's play with their reminiscence of the pedagogical setting of the school blackboard. The several instances of remediation involved—from the DM to the chalk graffiti to the quick media post—raise issues about the material dimensions of this kind of affective worldmaking. As examples of "inscriptive media, ... the representations they entail and circulate are crucially material as well as semiotic" (Gitelman 6). This materiality contributes to the agentive force of @CatcallsofGraz, whereby the collective consciousness-raising equally involves the respective victims of catcalling and allies against misogyny writ large. Like Jansma's efforts to track the ubiquity of catcalling and Jones's cultivation of love politics, *@CatcallsofGraz* circulates grievances and resistance strategies as part of a larger effort to denormalize street harassment and empower its victims. As an autobiographical practice that calls attention to the fact that "women will tend to face hostility of various kinds because they are women in a man's world (i.e., patriarchy)" (Manne 33), *@CatcallsofGraz* reclaims the public spaces in which harassment occurred and re-signifies them as platforms against sexism and misogyny. By citing the form of harassment directly, the chalk graffiti also validate the gravity of people's experience of catcalling. Rendering the insults visible "purports to speak a truth about lived experience and foster the forms of recognition we require for a more just politics and social field" (Poletti 6). Therefore, as texts, they enable a sense of recognition for a counterpublic which coheres around a shared sense of vulnerability and a shared commitment towards resistance. Therefore, *@CatcallsofGraz* can offer itself up as a communal space and activity to "chalk back" at catcallers and, by doing so, validates the vulnerability of those who have been publicly harassed. As feminist interventions, they may prompt readers' recognition through the affective potential of narrative worldmaking. As such, they facilitate the kinds of affirmative encounters that literary studies scholars such as Rita Felski attribute to literary texts. Felksi suggests that literary narratives "offer solace and relief not to be found elsewhere, confirming that I am not entirely alone, that there are others who think or feel like me. Through this experience of affiliation, I feel myself acknowledged; I am rescued from the fear of invisibility, from the terror of not being seen." (Felski 33)

While the global dimension of this project speaks to the ubiquity of harassment, the specific locations of the individual graffiti resonate particularly with those readers located in the same city. Being able to recognize the street corners and landmarks memorialized in the quick media posts is one way of being reminded of one's own positionality towards these texts; stumbling upon the chalk graffiti on the way home from work, or while walking a young child to school, makes them part of one's life, regardless of any prior affiliation to the Facebook or Instagram network. Although the experience of being catcalled is deeply gendered, the graffiti integrate the randomness and unpredictable content of catcalling into people's experience of the city, making it matter and a part of the materiality of everybody's life.

Conclusion

Through the circulation of affect, these quick media projects contribute to a kind of worldmaking that imagines a more just and equal society. The circulation of emancipatory narratives via quick media echoes Ahmed's definition of feminist interventions as "finding ways to exist in a world that makes it difficult to exist" (*Living a Feminist Life* 239). The volume of posts and tweets that detail experiences of public harassment not only shed light on these difficulties but also index emotionally taxing coping strategies. The dynamic and interactive responses to these quick media projects validate the incurred injustice and enter it into the public discourse around misogyny, both in the context of feminist counterpublics which protest such forms of systemic violence and sexist groups that downplay or condone them. Therefore, while quick media feminist interventions do not merely sketch utopian worlds devoid of public harassment, they affirm the agency of harassed individuals and groups and provide spaces to share grievances, offer care, and practice solidarity. The fact that they go viral, as so many of them do, is perhaps one of many steps towards a more just future. As Catherine MacKinnon proposes, regarding her idea of "butterfly politics," "the right small human intervention in an unstable political system can sooner or later have large complex reverberations" (MacKinnon: 1).

Bibliography

Ahmed, Sara. *Living a Feminist Life*. Duke UP, 2017.
——. *The Cultural Politics of Emotion*. Edinburgh UP, 2014.

——. "Affective Economies." *Social Text*, vol. 22, no.1, 2004, pp. 117–39.

Augenbraun, Eric. "Occupy Wall Street and the Limits of Spontaneous Street Protest." *The Guardian*, 29 September 2011, http://www.theg uardian.com/ commentisfree/cifamerica/2011/sep/29/occupy-wall-street-protest.

Bailey, Moya. *Misogynoir Transformed: Black Women's Digital Resistance.* New York UP, 2021.

——. "More on the Origin of Misogynoir." *Tumblr*, 27 April 2014, https://moyazb.tumblr.com/post/84048113369/more-on-the-origin-of-mi sofynoir.

boyd, danah. "Social Network Sites as Networked Publics: Affordances, Dynamics, and Implications." *A Networked Self: Identity, Community, and Culture on Social Network Sites*, edited by Zizi Papacharissi, Rout-ledge, 2011, pp. 39–58.

Boyle, Karen. *#MeToo, Weinstein, and Feminism.* Palgrave Macmillan, 2019.

Butler, Judith. *Excitable Speech: A Politics of the Performative.* Routledge, 1997.

Carr, David. "Hashtag Activism, and its Limits." *The New York Times*, 25 March 2012, https://www.nytimes.com/2012/03/26/business/media /hashtag-activism-and-its-limits.html.

Collins, Patricia Hill. *Black Sexual Politics: African Americans, Gender, and the New Racism.* Routledge, 2004.

Dadas, Caroline. "Hashtag Activism: The Promise and Risk of 'Atten-tion.'" *Social Writing/Social Media: Publics, Presentations, Pedagogies*, edited by Douglas M. Walls and Stephanie Vie, WAC, 2017, pp. 17–36.

Earl, Jennifer. "Protest Online: Theorizing the Consequences of On-line Engagement." *The Consequences of Social Movements*, edited by Lorenzo Bosi, Marco Giugni, and Katrin Uba, Cambridge UP, 2016, pp. 363–400.

Felski, Rita. *Uses of Literature.* Wiley Blackwell, 2008.

Fileborn, Bianca, and Rachel Loney-Howes, editors. *#MeToo and the Pol-itics of Social Change.* Palgrave Macmillan, 2019.

Friedman, May. *Mommyblogs and the Changing Face of Motherhood.* Uni-versity of Toronto Press, 2013.

——, and Silvia Schultermandl. Introduction. *Click and Kin: Transnational Identity and Quick Media*. University of Toronto Press, 2016, pp. 3–24.

Gitelman, Lisa. *Always Already New: Media, History, and the Data of Culture*. MIT Press, 2006.

Johnson, Paige. "You Ok Sis?": Black Vernacular, Community Formation, and the Innate Tensions of the Hashtag." *#identity: Hashtagging Race, Gender, Sexuality, and Nation*, edited by Abigail De Kosnik and Keith Feldman, University of Michigan Press, 2019, pp. 57–67.

MacKinnon, Catharine A. *Butterfly Politics: Changing the World for Women*. Harvard UP, 2019.

Manne, Kate. *Down Girl: The Logics of Misogyny*. Oxford UP, 2018.

McNeill, Laurie. "There Is No 'I' in Network: Social Networking Sites and Posthuman Auto/Biography." *Biography*, vol. 35, no. 1, 2012, pp. 65–82.

——, and John David Zuern, editors. "Online Lives 2.0: Introduction." *Online Lives 2.0*. Special issue of *Biography*, vol. 38, no. 2, 2015, pp. v–xlvi.

Nash, Jennifer C. "Practicing Love: Black Feminism, Love-Politics, and Post-Intersectionality." *Meridians*, vol. 11, no. 2, 2011, pp. 1–24.

Nakamura, Lisa. "Race and Identity in Digital Media." *Mass Media and Society*, 5th edition, edited by James Curran, Bloomsbury Academic, 2010, pp. 336–347.

——, and Peter Cow-White, editors. *Race After the Internet*. Routledge, 2011.

Noble, Safiya Umoja. *Algorithms of Oppression: How Search Engines Reinforce Racism*. New York UP, 2018.

Noble, Safiya Umoja, and Brendesha M. Tynes. *The Intersectional Internet: Race, Sex, Class and Culture Online*. Peter Lang, 2016.

Paasonen, Susanna. "Resonant Networks: On Affect and Social Media." In *Public Sphere of Resonance: Constellations of Affect and Language*, edited by Anne Fleig and Christian von Scheve. Routledge, 2020, pp. 49–62.

Papacharissi, Zizi. *Affective Publics: Sentiment, Technology, and Politics*. Oxford UP, 2015.

———. *A Networked Self: Identity, Community, and Culture on Social Network Sites*. Routledge, 2011.

Poletti, Anna. *Stories of the Self: Life Writing After the Book*. New York UP, 2020.

———, and Julie Rak, editors. *Identity Technologies: Constructing the Self Online*. University of Wisconsin Press, 2014.

Warner, Michael. "Public and Counterpublics." *Public Culture*, vol.14, no. 1, 2002, pp. 49–90.

Zimmerman, Tegan. "#Intersectionality: The Fourth Wave Feminist Twitter Community." *Atlantis*, vol. 38, no. 1, 2017, pp. 54–70.

Mediated Narratives as Companions

Ahmet Atay

Narratives are what keep me connected and alive at this particular cultural and historical moment. Mediated stories are part of my everyday reality, as my every day has become increasingly more mediated and fragmented due to the COVID-19 pandemic. As a global citizen who lives alone, I used to travel between countries and maneuver around cultures, visit home (Cyprus), and spend some time with my relatives. I was able to simultaneously belong to bigger urban and small rural settings, spending enough time in each to work, live, escape, and belong. Travelling presented opportunities for creating and exchanging stories, as well as listening to stories from home. Travelling also meant returning home and connecting with my family. Travelling has not only allowed me to return, to step into my past and aspects of my identity that come to life in that particular context, but it has also provided different ways of imagining and performing my own cultural identity. Similarly, stories as an act, performance, and exchange contribute to worldmaking, where I make sense of aspects of my identities, creating and recreating different identity performances. Since March 2020, I have been home-bound, living in a small rural Ohio town and experiencing the world around me through mediated narratives. These days, my stories are limited to and revolve around my apartment, its four walls, my cat Plum, short walks that I take to breathe, and the endless cyber-meetings I regularly attend. In this essay, I utilize my personal experiences to theorize mediated narratives as companions, friends, lifelines, and ways to experience the world.

Narratives are integral to human communication. According to Walter Fisher, "humans are essentially storytellers" (7). We use oral, written, and visual stories to communicate, make sense of who we are, explain the world around us, and archive our experiences. Donald E. Polkinghorne posits that "narrative is a form of meaning making" (36). Paul John Eakin argues that "[w]e tell stories about ourselves every day" (1). Hence, we use and embody narratives to story and represent our identities. We tell stories about home and belonging (Chawla); we tell stories about coming out (Adams); we tell stories about transnational diasporic experiences (Atay, "Digital Diasporic Experiences"; Atay, "Journey of Errors"); and we tell stories to decolonize narrative methods (Bhattacharya; Chawla). We tell stories to live.

In the last several months, due to the COVID-19 pandemic, both locally and globally, all of us around the world have been more isolated than at any point in recent human history. People have experienced localized or individualized isolations due to social distancing, lockdowns, the encroaching presence of remote and online work environments, and the fear of domestic and international travel. Globally, the COVID-19 pandemic has created new borders and boundaries, restrictions, fears of movement and people, and finally, new limitations of access and face-to-face communication. I think the pandemic and our attempts to combat the harsh and deadly reality of the virus have caused new realities to emerge, such as having less human contact, even with family members and close friends. While our interactions have diminished, the pandemic simultaneously brought with it new perspectives on the role and importance of stories in our lives. As human contact deteriorated in our lives, we could turn to written and mediated stories to find solace and to feel connected. In the following narrative, I present a personal story to illuminate the ways in which narratives, particularly mediated narratives, function in the absence of mundane and routine everyday life encounters or communication. Hence, I argue that stories can function as companions.

Beginning of the Story

Since March 2020, I have chosen not to interact with people face-to-face not only to protect myself but also others, by minimizing the risk of transmission of COVID-19. As a transnational diasporic being, I teach at a small university in a small rural town in Ohio. Thus, I live away from relatively bigger cities, such as Akron, Canton, or Cleveland. I was already feeling isolated when the dark winter blanketed us early last winter. Due to high numbers of infections and deaths, we went to the shelter-in-place phase for days during late March and early April. Although the spring and then the summer arrived, fear of the virus kept my social bubble very small, and I only communicated in person with a couple of people. I was isolated and living alone in my already lonely story. I often joke that being an international student and faculty member prepared me well for these isolating conditions, as I was not always able to travel to visit my family during the breaks, due to previous personal circumstances (such as dedicating break-time to research) and geographical distances. Therefore, as a student, I was often stuck in dorm rooms or my small apartments while others were traveling to visit their families for holidays or summer breaks. I remember one cold winter when I was studying in Iowa, I spent the winter break in my dorm room. I was one of the very few students residing in a big and old Victorian-style building. It was a very cold winter often hit by snowstorms. To pass the time and cope with loneliness, I read academic books and novels and watched films and soap operas. Since I did not have a car, I was unable to drive. Instead, a friend of mine from Japan and I regularly visited a coffee shop that was only a block or two from my dorm to break the routine and socialize. At the time, I did not have a personal computer; we had to take turns using one of the two computers in the lobby. Therefore, I depended on books, films, and television to survive. In many ways, such experiences prepared me well for isolation.

I begin my story with this interlude, not to say that I survived before and can therefore do it again, but to show a pattern that persists in my life. Namely, mediated stories function as my companion in isolation or when I travel to destinations where I know practically no one. Films, television shows, serial narratives, such as soap operas or novels, and online platforms provide continuity and connection, but they are also a way to escape, to feel less isolated and lonely. During this pandemic, as I hardly ever interact with other people in the regular sense, my only connections with them are through mediated forms. I teach my classes through Microsoft Teams, I regularly attend endless meetings on Zoom or Teams, I talk to my family on Skype, and I text with friends or communicate on Facebook messenger. They are part of the everyday stories that I create, and they are characters in my stories that I share with others. They are my mediated family members, friends, students, and colleagues.

One day resembles another when you are in isolation during a pandemic, especially if you live alone. At some point, your memory may fail you, and you cannot really remember or distinguish one day in May from another in September. You might recall the films you watched or novels you read, but your day will be blurry because you don't really have a cohesive story to tell or remember. Your soap operas or television series mark the days and help you separate one from another. This was one of those days—the story within the story.

November 2020

It was one of those days when you wake up to a cold morning. Your cat gently presses his paws on your nose and plays with your beard. You don't want to get out of bed and start the day because there is a full day ahead of you. You would rather curl up in bed with a good mystery novel than attend a number of meetings and teach your classes. You know that your students are tired because you are tired. They are dispersed all around the world, coming into your virtual classroom to learn and to feel that they belong to an educational community. It is clear that they are struggling to get through the semester because their emails ask for extensions on their assignments or tell you about their positive COVID-19 status. You finally convince yourself to get out of bed. You yield to your cat's demand for food and make a cup of coffee to wake yourself up. It is cold; the grass is covered with frost. You turn up the heat in your apartment and sit in front of your computer. You check your emails and look at the news to catch up with US politics and see what is happening in Europe and at home. The latest Brexit news annoys you, and you are already fed up with the ongoing US election process. You ignore your emails because you are not ready to attend to them. You decide to watch an old film to keep you company as you eat your breakfast. You admire Ginger Rogers's acting, as she reminds you of films you watched when you were a child. When you are an only child, movies and novels become your companions. Once the film is over, you are ready at last to start the day. It is already 9:30 am.

You have a short meeting with a student who is failing your class. He cries, and you want to cry with him. You tell him that you cannot write his papers for him and that he must try a bit harder, even though the times are tough. You have another meeting at 10 am, the content of which bores you so much that you start reading and answering your emails. When that meeting is over, you log in to your next meeting. You realize that you are wearing your gray sweater to look presentable and a colorful pajama bottom. They reflect your fluctuating mood because you are overbooked with meetings, and you want to attend to your class preparation. You manage to eat your lunch while you talk to your parents on Zoom. They give you a quick update on their day. They keep you sane and provide a consistent routine. You hang up and run to your 1 pm meeting. Once the meeting is over, you teach two classes back-to-back. You plan to take a walk in between, but you've run out of time.

Once the classes are done at 5 pm, you run out of your apartment for a quick walk and to try to catch the end of the daylight. You feel cold and return home to find your cat waiting for you in the front window. He is hungry and wants to smell you as you walk in. You feed him, check and respond to your emails, and talk to your friend on the phone while preparing your dinner. He tells you that he has an evening meeting, and you both hang up. You eat your dinner while you watch one of your soap operas. You realize that you don't like Gabi, and Claire really annoys you. Gabi reminds you of one of your co-workers—maybe that's why you don't like her. You realize it is 7:30 pm, and you rush to attend to your schoolwork. At 9 pm, you make a cup of coffee to keep you from passing out from fatigue. You tune in to watch another soap opera, and you cry over Sharon's cancer storyline. You hate health-related stories because you fear losing family members while you are away. You remember meeting Sharon as a character in the late 1990s when you were in Cyprus. You remind yourself that, in a way, you two have grown up together. She is your friend, at least that's what you think.

By 10 pm, you curl up on your couch to read your new mystery novel. It is the first in a 12-installment series. It takes place in a small Midwest town that reminds you of your own. It is a cozy mystery, so you read it to be entertained and to keep yourself company. You don't care for the characters yet, but you know that, over time, you will get to know them intimately, as the authors narrate their personal turbulences. You realize that these novels all have funny titles. You chuckle, and it wakes up your cat. He looks at you with wondering eyes while you return to your book. Incoming text messages interrupt your reading, and you briefly chat with your friends from graduate school. By 11 pm, you decide to catch up with your British soap operas. Even though you are two years behind, you hope that you can catch up. You realize how much you miss the UK and Europe, but you have no means of travel at the moment. You watch the adventures of your favorite characters. You don't like going to bed early, so you decide to watch another film. The old movies from 1940 that you choose to watch give you some consistency. You start noticing patterns among them when you watch all the films you can find from a particular year. You realize that the war in Europe influenced the stories in most of these films. The sets, patterns, fashions of the year, songs, and stories give you comfort and consistency. By 1 am, you realize that you have been looking at screens since 7:15 am, and it is time to go to bed. You curl up in your bed, listening to the blowing wind and feeling the warmth of your cat, as he sleeps next to your feet. You feel grateful that you adopted him three years ago and that he is part of your everyday narrative.

End of the Story

In the absence of face-to-face human interactions, the inability to get together with friends, and the lack of means to visit family, mediated narratives and communication with people on cyber platforms have become the way of life. Communication through cyberspace and mediated narratives became my everyday story. As the days blurred and the boundaries between workplace and personal life disappeared, increased communication with students and colleagues in cyberspace also became very taxing. In this reality, one more meeting meant another hour in front of my computer screen. Looking at the last several months collectively, I quickly realize that I don't have any stories to tell except nonstop meetings and my limited online communication with friends and family. My story is stuck between my four walls, and in the absence of human interactions in the physical sense, all I have are mediated stories that I take part in or watch every day to feel connected. Hence, mediated stories are my stories. I enjoy the stories of my favorite soap opera characters and replace my small-town living with those in mystery novels. These characters stand in as my friends, as I allow their stories to intersect with mine. They offer me an escape but also provide friendship and a sense of belonging. Mediated narratives perform the necessary function of providing me companionship and connection but also keep me alive during these isolating times.

Bibliography

Adams, Tony E. *Narrating the Closet*. Left Coast Press, 2011.

Atay, Ahmet. "Digital Diasporic Experiences in Digital Queer Spaces." *Click and Kin: Transnational Identity and Quick Media*, edited by May Friedman and Silvia Schultermandl, University of Toronto Press, 2016, pp. 139–158.

——. "Journey of Errors: Finding Home in Academia." *Cultural Studies ↔ Critical Methodologies*, vol. 18, no. 1, 2018, pp. 16–22.

Bhattacharya, Kakali. "Coloring Memories and Immigrations of 'Home': Crafting a De/Colonizing Autoethnography." *Cultural Studies ↔ Critical Methodologies*, vol. 18, no. 1, 2018, pp. 9–15.

Chawla, Devika. "Walk, Walking, Talking, Home." *Handbook of Autoethnography*, edited by Stacy Holman Jones, Tony E. Adams, and Carolyn Ellis, Left Coast Press, 2013, pp. 162–172.

——., and Ahmet Atay. "Introduction: Decolonizing Autoethnography." *Cultural Studies ↔ Critical Methodologies*, vol. 18, no. 1, 2018, pp. 3–8.

Eakin, Paul John. *Living Autobiographically: How We Create Identity in Narrative*. Cornell UP, 2008.

Fisher, Walter. "Narration as Human Communication Paradigm: The Case of Public Morale Argument." *Communication Monographs*, vol. 51, no. 1, 1984, pp. 1–22.

Polkinghorne, Donald E. *Narrative Knowing and the Human Sciences*. State University of New York Press, 1988.

"Plan B"

Damir Arsenijević, Šejla Šehabović and Marko Gačnik (translated by Tag McEntegart)

PLAN B

AND THEN, THEY CAME FROM INDIA. BOUGHT THE FACTORY. THEY EXTRACT PROFIT, THEY DISREGARD THE LAWS. THE STATE OFFICIALS TURNING A BLIND EYE.

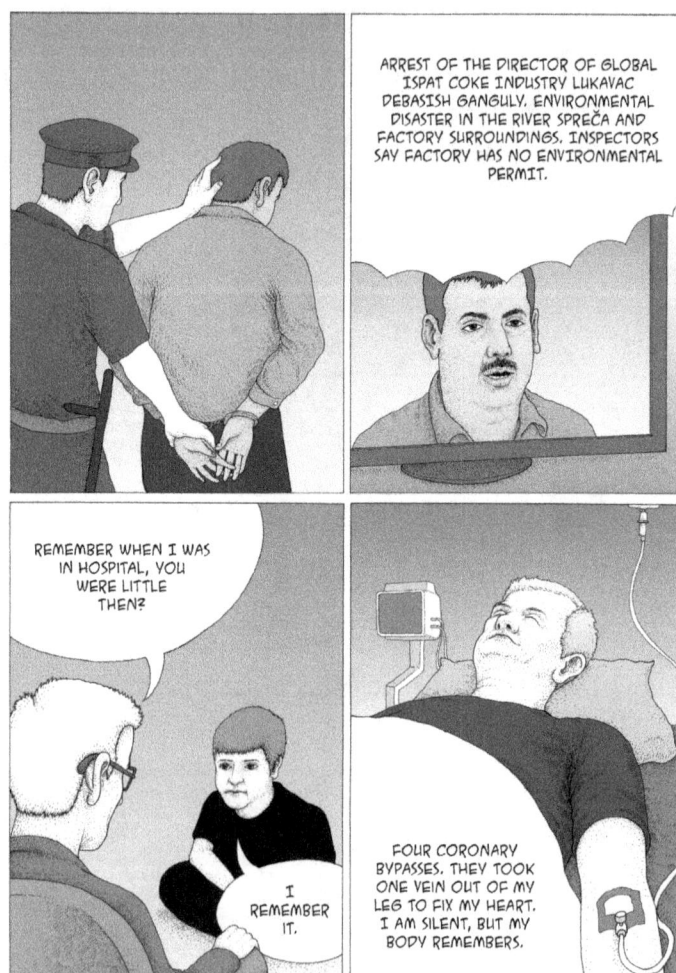

INDIAN-BRITISH BILLIONAIRE PRAMOD MITTAL ARRESTED TOGETHER WITH DIRECTOR PARAMESH BHATACHARI. FORMER GIKIL DIRECTOR DEBASISH GANGULY IS AT LARGE.

THEY'RE ALL GOING TO GET AWAY WITH IT, SON. THERE ARE TIMES WHEN I AM GLAD YOU DON'T LIVE IN BOSNIA. THE FACTORY NOW EMPLOYS A HANDFUL OF PEOPLE. THE OWNERS BOUGHT IT FOR PITTANCE. THEY NEVER HONOURED THE CONTRACT THEY SIGNED. THEY CAUSED ECOLOGICAL DISASTERS. THE STATE OFFICIALS KEEP SILENT AND PROMISE CRUMBS TO THE WORKERS. AND THERE ARE FEWER AND FEWER WORKERS LEFT.

LET'S HEAR THAT STORY ABOUT THE GOAT AGAIN, GRANDPA!

THE WHOLE OF TUZLA MILKED ONE GOAT?

THERE ARE MANY STORIES ABOUT THE TUZLA GOAT.

"Plan B" is a chapter from the graphic novel Zemlja–voda–zrak (2020, Earth–Water–Air, translated by Tag McEntegart), edited by Damir Arsenijević, written by Šejla Šehabović, and illustrated by Marko Gačnik.

Gender, Affect, and Politics:
A Three-Part Radio Series

Contributors

Ahmet Atay is Associate Professor of Communication at the College of Wooster. His research focuses on diasporic experiences and cultural identity formations; political and social complexities of city life, such as immigrant and queer experiences; the usage of new media technologies in different settings; the notion of home; and representation of different identity formations in media and film texts. He is the author of *Globalization's Impact on Identity Formation: Queer Diasporic Males in Cyberspace* (2015) and the co-editor of 13 books. His scholarship has appeared in a number of journals and edited books.

Jana Aresin is a Doctoral Researcher at the American Studies Institute at Friedrich-Alexander University Erlangen-Nuernberg. She studied Japanese and Migration Studies at Leipzig University and the University of Copenhagen. In 2020-21, she was an Elisabeth-List Junior Fellow at the Coordination Centre for Gender Studies and Equal Opportunity at the University of Graz. Her research interest is the cultural and media history of the early Cold War period (1945-1960) in comparative perspective, with a regional focus on the United States and Japan. She is a member of the research projects "Reeducation Revisited: Transnational and Comparative Perspectives on the Post-World War II Period in the US, Japan, and Germany" and the "Global Sentimentality Project."

Damir Arsenijević is Full Professor of Anglo-American Literatures and Cultures at the Department of English, University of Tuzla, Bosnia and Herzegovina. He is a literary theorist and a psychoanalyst in training with the San Francisco Bay Area Lacanian School of Psychoanalysis. In 2011/12, he was a Fulbright Visiting Professor in the Department of Rhetoric, University of California at Berkeley, and between 2013/2016, he was a Leverhulme Fellow at De Montfort University, Leicester, UK. He works at the intersection of arts-academia-activism throughout the geographic and affective area of Yugoslavia. He is founder of the first platform for environmental humanities in Bosnia and Herzegovina *Zemlja-Voda-Zrak* (www.zemljavodazrak.com) that gathers individuals, communities, and initiatives throughout this country that productively intervene in cases of environmental violence for protection and defense of the commons. His latest book is *Unbribable Bosnia and Herzegovina: The Fight for The Commons* (Nomos Verlag, 2015).

Adisa Bašić has published five collections of poetry: *Eve's sentences* (Omnibus 1999), *Trauma Market* (Omnibus 2004), *Promo Clip for My Homeland* (Dobra knjiga 2010), *Motel of Unknown Heroes* (Dobra knjiga 2014) and *Nettle Tree* (Planjax 2020), as well as the book of short stories *Until Tomorrow, Then: Stories about Love and Marriage* (Buybook, 2017). Her poems have been included in all recent anthologies and selections of Bosnian poetry. She defended her doctoral dissertation entitled "Comic Approach to Erotic Love in Selected South Slavic Lyric Poetry," under the mentorship of professor Renate Hansen-Kokoruš, in November 2019 at the University of Graz. She teaches poetry and creative writing at the Faculty of Philosophy in Sarajevo. Adisa Bašić regularly participates in literary evenings, festivals, and panel discussions in the country and abroad. She has won a number of domestic and foreign literary awards as well as scholarships for writers in Austria, Germany, and the United States.

Claudia Breger is the Villard Professor of German and Comparative Literature at Columbia University, New York. Having received her PhD and Habilitation from Humboldt University, Berlin, she taught at the University of Paderborn, Germany, and Indiana University, Bloomington, before joining Columbia in 2017. Her research and teaching focus on modern and contemporary culture, with emphases on film, performance, literature, and literary and cultural theory, as well as the intersections of gender, sexuality, and race. Her most recent book, *Making Worlds: Affect and Collectivity in Contemporary European Cinema*, was published by Columbia University Press in 2020.

Ann Cvetkovich is currently Director of the Pauline Jewett Institute of Women's and Gender Studies at Carleton University in Ottawa, Ontario, Canada. Until 2019, she was Ellen Clayton Garwood Centennial Professor of English and Professor of Women's and Gender Studies at the University of Texas at Austin. She is the author of *Mixed Feelings: Feminism, Mass Culture, and Victorian Sensationalism* (Rutgers, 1992); *An Archive of Feelings: Trauma, Sexuality, and Lesbian Public Cultures* (Duke, 2003); and *Depression: A Public Feeling* (Duke, 2012). She co-edited (with Ann Pellegrini) "Public Sentiments," a special issue of *The Scholar and Feminist Online*, and (with Janet Staiger and Ann Reynolds) *Political Emotions* (Routledge, 2010). She is coeditor, with Annamarie Jagose, of *GLQ: A Journal of Lesbian and Gay Studies*. Her ongoing writing projects focus on the current state of LGBTQ archives and the creative use of them by artists to create counterarchives and interventions in public history.

May Friedman's research looks at unstable identities, including bodies that do not conform to traditional racial and national or aesthetic lines. May blends social work, teaching, research, writing and parenting, and her passions include social justice and reality TV (she is firmly in favor of living with contradiction). Recent publications include explorations of fat and fertility, reproduction and parenting, examinations of fat temporalities, and writing on the intersections of family and social media platforms such as Instagram.

Marko Gačnik was born and raised in Sarajevo, Bosnia and Herzegovina. Since early age and in elementary school he showed interest in drawing and visual arts, which led him to enroll in the local high school of applied arts. After that, he attained a bachelor degree in graphic design at the Academy of Fine Arts in Sarajevo. Following his formal education, he started working in smaller design businesses and marketing agencies, mostly creating visual identities, brand merchandise and web ads. Nowadays, he works as a freelance designer and illustrator, mostly cooperating with fellow artists, writers and musicians. Work on illustrations led him to start drawing comics and storyboards.

Renate Hansen-Kokoruš is a retired professor of Slavic literatures and cultures (up to 2019) at the Dep. of Slavic Studies at the University of Graz (Austria), after having affiliations in Mannheim, Berlin, Waterloo (Can.), Zadar, Frankfurt/M and Innsbruck. Her research topics are satire and humor, the chronotope of the return in South Slavic literatures, space of Siberia and Russia, identity in literature and film, gender and intertextuality in South Slavic literatures. She is co-editor of the journal *Anzeiger für Slavische Philologie* and editor of the book series *Grazer Studien zur Slawistik* (Dr. Kovač). With Darko Lukić and Boris Senker, she published *Satire und Komik in der bosnisch-herzegowinischen, kroatischen, montenegrinischen und serbischen Literatur* (Dr. Kovač, 2018) and, with Olaf Terpitz, *Jewish Literatures and Cultures in Southeastern Europe* (Böhlau/Brill, 2021). Other recent articles are dedicated to social critics, utopia and satire in Croatian detective stories and film, space in Dostoevsky, gender presentations, memory and trauma.

Iveta Jansová holds an MA in Cultural Studies and a Ph.D. in Media and Cultural Studies at Palacký University in Olomouc. After the completion of her Ph.D., she took up the positions of Assistant Professor and coordinator of audiovisual courses at the Department of Media Studies and Journalism at Masaryk University, Brno, Czech Republic. Her main research interests are audience studies, fan studies, and representations of gender in the media, mainly in the crime genre.

Tag (Mary) McEntegart is a specialist in educational communication who has been involved in work in the countries of former Yugoslavia for nearly 25 years. She lives in Coventry, UK, a city that was almost destroyed in November 1940 by German bombing. In the aftermath, the city twinned itself with all cities worldwide that had suffered such destruction—including Sarajevo and Belgrade. Coventry's Belgrade Theatre is called the Belgrade Theatre because the joint trades unions of Yugoslavia made a gift of timber which the City Council determined would be used to build a theatre. Here, starting in 1965, a new educational theatre form emerged that came to be called Theatre in Education. From its outset, the TIE Team at the Belgrade pioneered environmental education. She has worked as an English-language copy editor and co-translator on a range of texts, across different genres, written in Bosnian, Croatian, and Serbian.

Deborah D.E.E.P. Mouton is an internationally known writer, educator, activist, performer, and Poet Laureate Emeritus of Houston, Texas. Formerly ranked the #2 Best Female Performance Poet in the World, her most recent poetry collection, Newsworthy, garnered her a Pushcart nomination and was named a finalist for the 2019 Writer's League of Texas Book Award and an honorable mention for the Summerlee Book Prize. A German translation, under the title "Berichtenswert," was released in Fall 2021 by Elif Verlag. As a finalist for Texas State Poet Laureate, a Kennedy Center Citizen fellowship, and the prestigious Breadloaf Retreat, her work has been highlighted and studied in Canada, England, New Zealand, and Germany. She lives and creates in Houston, TX. For more information visitwww.LiveLifedeep.com.

Heike Paul is Chair of American Studies at Friedrich-Alexander-University Erlangen-Nuernberg and director of the Bavarian American Academy in Munich. She received her degrees from Goethe University Frankfurt and Leipzig University. In 2018, she was recipient of the Gottfried Wilhelm Leibniz Prize of the German Research Foundation, and she has been a member of the Bavarian American Academy of Sciences and Humanities since 2019. She held fellowships at Harvard University, the Institute for Advanced Study (*Wissenschaftskolleg*) in Berlin, the IFUSS at the University of Illinois Urbana-Champaign, Graz University, and the Thomas Mann House in Los Angeles. Twice, she was Visiting Harris Professor at Dartmouth College. Among her publications are *The Myths That Made America* (2014), *Understanding Stewart O'Nan* (2020), and *Amerikanischer Staatsbürgersentimentalismus*

(2021). She has published widely on cultural mobility, reeducation, critical regionalism, gender studies, populism, and sentimentality. She currently leads the "Global Sentimentality Project" at FAU.

Jelena Petrović is an art researcher, theorist and curator. She is (co)author of texts, events, exhibitions and projects related to new epistemological models of art(-theory) production dealing with issues of war and violence, critical and human geography, the politics of affects and the politics of error. From 2008 to 2014, she was an active member of the art-theory group *Grupa Spomenik* (The Monument Group); she is also co-founder and member of the feminist curatorial collective *Red Min(e)d* (redmined.org). As an initiator of the course *Living Archive: Feminist Curatorship and Contemporary Artistic Practices*, she was a lecturer at the Academy of Fine Arts and Design, University of Ljubljana (2014-2017). At the Academy of Fine Arts Vienna, she was appointed as the *Endowed Professor for Central and South Eastern European Art Histories* (2015-2017). Currently, she is working on her research project at the Academy of Fine Arts Vienna: *The Politics of Belonging-Art Geographies* (FWF Elise Richter Program 2019-2023).

Mirza Purić is a literary translator, free lector, and musician.

Silvia Schultermandl is Chair of American Studies at the University of Münster. She is the author of *Transnational Matrilineage: Mother-Daughter Conflicts in Asian American Literature* (2009) and *Ambivalent Transnational Belonging in American Literature* (2021) and co-editor of seven collections of essays which explore various themes in transnational studies, American literature and culture, as well as family and kinship studies. Her articles have appeared in the following journals, among others: Meridians, Atlantic Studies, Interactions, Journal of Transnational American Studies, and Journal of American Culture. She is currently developing the Palgrave Series in Kinship, Representation, and Difference and is embarking on a new project on kinship and social media. Her areas of interest include affect theory, literary theory, critical race theory, queer theory, visual culture, and transnational feminism.

Šejla Šehabović obtained her Bachelor and Master degrees in Literary Studies from the University of Tuzla. She has been a recipient of several literary awards and fellowships. She is the Director of the Museum of Literature and Performing Arts of Bosnia and Herzegovina in Sarajevo. Her books include: *Nőnem, többes szám*, Ex Libris, Budapest (2012)—translation from Bosnian to Hungarian by Viktória Radics; *Opowieści, rodzaj żeński, liczba mnoga*, Ad Publik Warszawa, (2012); *Make up*, Ad Publik, Warszawa, (2012); *Car Trojan ma kozie uszy*, Kraków, Maximum (2011)—translation from Bosnian to Polish by Agnieszka Żuchowska-Arendt; *Priče, ženski rod, množina* (2007), Nezavisne novine, Banjaluka; *Car Trojan ima kozije uši* (2005), Zoro, Zagreb/Sarajevo; and *Make up* (2004), Zoro, Zagreb/Sarajevo.

Dijana Simić (she/her) is a lecturer of Bosnian, Croatian, and Serbian literary and cultural studies in the Department of Slavic Studies at the University of Graz. As a Marietta-Blau-fellow, she conducted research at the Central European University in Budapest and the Universities of Banja Luka, Sarajevo, and Tuzla (2017). As an Elisabeth-List-fellow, she worked at the Coordination Center for Gender Studies at the University of Graz (2020-2021). Currently, she is completing her PhD project on gender, sexuality, and intimate counterpublics in recent Bosnian-Herzegovinian prose. Her teaching and research focus on Migration, Gender, and Memory Studies in the Former Yugoslav context.

Si Sophie Pages Whybrew, pronouns "she/her" or "they/them," is currently a Senior Scientist for Gender & Diversity Studies at the University of Music and Performing Arts Graz. In early 2021, she completed her dissertation on "Affective Trans worldmaking in Contemporary Science Fiction" at the University of Graz. From 2020-2021, she was an Elisabeth-List Junior Fellow in the research project "Literary Negotiations of Affective and Gendered Belongings" at the Coordination Centre for Gender Studies.

Index

GPSR Authorized Representative: Easy Access System Europe, Mustamäe tee 50, 10621 Tallinn, Estonia, gpsr.requests@easproject.com

www.ingramcontent.com/pod-product-compliance
Lightning Source LLC
Chambersburg PA
CBHW061731120626
46550CB00005B/1764